MARY W. CRAIG is a writer and his... and a graduate of the University ordinary people and how they live tics and economics of the elite. M: on various aspects of Scottish and ....ory to community groups across the country. Some historians are known as hedge-hogs, happily snuffling about rooting out the minutest of historical details. Others are known as eagles, soaring on high they see great vistas of historical events. A few are known as magpies: if something shiny and interesting catches their eye, they will try to capture it where possible. Mary is a magpie.

Borders Witch Hunt

17th Century Witchcraft Trials in the Scottish Borders

MARY W. CRAIG

Luath Press Limited
EDINBURGH
www.luath.co.uk

First published 2020
This edition 2022
Reprinted 2023, 2024

ISBN: 978-1-80425-009-9

Printed and bound by Clays Ltd., Bungay

Typeset in 10.5 point Sabon by Lapiz

Speed Southern Scotland below Marches 17th century map
© Reproduced with the permission of the National Library
of Scotland

Contents

Acknowledgements

THIS BOOK WAS written in an attempt to cast light on the social history surrounding the witchcraft trials that took place in the Scottish Borders in the 17th century. Much has been written about the phenomenon of witchcraft in Scotland but the combination of events and beliefs that occurred and held sway in the Scottish Borders give the trials there a particular identity and they remain an area for much study.

The records held at the National Records of Scotland and the National Library of Scotland have proved invaluable in compiling this book, as has the University of Edinburgh's Survey of Scottish Witchcraft and the Scottish Borders Archive service in Hawick. I wish to thank the Museum of Witchcraft in Boscastle, Cornwall, for the use of several woodcut images and general background information. Further thanks are due to Rhiannon Hunt who supplied the other illustrative artwork in this book and Mike and Jessica Troughton for their photographs. Finally, thanks are due to the editorial team at Luath Press for their help in producing this book.

Mary W. Craig

Note

SOME OF THE following chapters contain descriptions of crowd reactions. Some of these descriptions come directly from contemporary records, others are imagined responses based on those contemporary records.

The geographical area covered by this book constitutes the Scottish Borders region today. This did not exist in the 17th century. Some of the land in the north was, at that time, part of Midlothian while the southern border with England remained debatable for a large part of its length. Galashiels was known as Gallowshiels in the 17th century.

Summis desiderantes affectibus

The *summis desiderantes affectibus* (desiring with supreme ardour) was a Papal Bull regarding witchcraft issued by Pope Innocent VIII on 5 December 1484. The Bull was written in response to a request by the Dominican Inquisitor Heinrich Kramer for the authority to prosecute witchcraft in Germany after he was refused assistance by the local ecclesiastical authorities. The Bull did not confer any new powers but ratified the existing authority the Inquisition held to prosecute witches. It gave approval for the Inquisition to proceed 'correcting, imprisoning, punishing and chastising' such persons as it deemed guilty and urged local authorities to cooperate with the inquisitors and threatened those who impeded their work with excommunication.

'It being known that many persons of both sexes, unmindful of their own salvation and straying from the Catholic Faith, have abandoned themselves to devils, incubi and succubi, and by their incantations, spells, conjurations, and other accursed charms and crafts, enormities and horrid offences, have slain infants yet in the mother's womb, as also the offspring of cattle, have blasted the produce of the earth, the grapes of the vine, the fruits of the trees, nay, men and women, beasts of burden, herd-beasts, as well as animals of other kinds, vineyards, orchards, meadows, pasture-land, corn, wheat, and all other cereals; these wretches furthermore afflict and torment men and women, beasts of burden, herd-beasts, as well as animals of other kinds, with terrible and piteous pains and sore diseases, both internal and external; they hinder men from performing the sexual act and women from conceiving, whence husbands cannot know their wives nor wives receive their husbands; over and above this, they blasphemously renounce that Faith which is theirs by the Sacrament of Baptism, and at the instigation of the Enemy of Mankind they do not shrink from committing and perpetrating the foulest abominations and filthiest excesses to the deadly peril of their own souls, whereby they outrage the Divine Majesty and are a cause of scandal and danger to very many.' Papal Bull of Pope Innocent VIII, 1484[1]

Timeline of events

1484 Pope Innocent VIII published his Papal Bull against witches

1563 Scottish Witchcraft Act passed

1564 John Knox declares witches to be enemies of God

1590 North Berwick witches attempt to drown King James VI

1597 King James VI publishes his great book on witchcraft, *Daemonologie*

1600 Plague in the Borders

1607 Plague in the Borders

1623 Famine in the Borders

1624 Plague in the Borders

1625 King Charles I marries Henrietta Maria, a French Catholic and issues the Act of Revocation in Scotland, revoking all gifts of royal or church land made to the nobility

1630 Plague in the Borders

1635 Plague and famine in the Borders

1637 Charles attempts to impose Anglican services on the Presbyterian Church of Scotland; Jenny Geddes starts riots at St Giles Cathedral, Edinburgh

1638 Signing of the National Covenant in Scotland

1639 First Bishops' War

1640 General Assembly passes the First Condemnatory Act against witches

1640 Second Bishops' War

1643 General Assembly passes the Second Condemnatory Act against witches

1644 General Assembly passes the Third Condemnatory Act against witches

1644 Scottish Civil War

1644 Plague and famine in the Borders

1645 General Assembly passes the Fourth Condemnatory Act against witches

1645 Battle of Philiphaugh outside Selkirk
1648 Famine in the Borders
1649 General Assembly passes the Fifth Condemnatory Act against witches
1649 Execution of King Charles I
1649 Cromwell invades Scotland
1675 Famine in the Borders
1677-1682 A number of prominent members of the aristocracy in the court of Louis XIV at Versailles were sentenced on charges of poisoning and witchcraft
1692 Salem witch trials in Salem, Massachusetts
1695 Famine in the Borders
1700 Last witch executed in the Borders
1722 Last witch executed in Scotland
1736 The Scottish Witchcraft Act was formally repealed by Parliament and replaced with the Witchcraft Act of Great Britain which placed much greater emphasis on real proofs and evidence
1773 The Divines of the Associated Presbytery of Scotland passed a resolution affirming their belief in witchcraft
1944 Trial of Helen Duncan, known as Hellish Nell, the last person to be imprisoned under the Witchcraft Act
1950s A series of investigations and hearings chaired by Senator Joseph McCarthy were held in an effort to expose the supposed communist infiltration of various areas of the US Government; became known as a 'witchunt'
1952 Arthur Miller's play The Crucible used the Salem witch trials as a metaphor for McCarthyism
2003 Around 750 people are killed as witches in Assam and West Bengal, India
2006-2008 Between 25,000 and 50,000 children in Kinshasa, Democratic Republic of the Congo, accused of witchcraft Fawza Falih Muhammad Ali was condemned to death for practising witchcraft
2008 President Kikwete of Tanzania publicly condemned witchdoctors for killing albinos for their body parts, which are thought to bring good luck; at least 25 albinos have been murdered between March 2007 and 2017

At least 11 people accused of witchcraft were burned to death by a mob in Kenya

More than 50 people were killed in two Highlands provinces of Papua New Guinea for allegedly practising witchcraft

2010 Amah Hemmah was accused of witchcraft and burned to death in Ghana

2011 Amina Bint Abdulhalim Nassar was beheaded for practising witchcraft and sorcery in Saudi Arabia

2012 Muree bin Ali Al Asiri was beheaded on charges of sorcery and witchcraft in Saudi Arabia

2013 69 reported cases of accusations of women performing witchcraft in Nepal

2019 In Fijia, a father blamed witchcraft for the death of his family

Introduction

17TH CENTURY SCOTLAND started with plague and ended with famine and, between those two events, the lives of nobles and peasants were turned upside down. The crowns of Scotland and England were united; a King lost his head; men the length of the British Isles went to war over the correct form of worship; a monarchy was turned into a republic and back again and the form of parliamentary rule was changed out of all recognition. Faced with apparent chaos and the breakdown of the natural order of things, a wave of fear and hysteria travelled across the countryside that resulted in hundreds of accusations of witchcraft.

This witch hysteria was greatest in Scotland and the towns and villages of the Scottish Borders in particular saw local men and women accused and sentenced to be worriet (strangled) to death and their bodies burned. Trials were conducted in all four of the Border counties: Berwickshire, Peebleshire, Selkirkshire and Roxburghshire. In towns and villages alike, accusations generated by fear, hysteria and, in some cases, malice were made, investigations held and victims worriet and burned.

The total numbers of those who died may never be fully known but piecing together what records exist between 1600 and 1700, some 352 known trials of witches took place in the Borders area which resulted in 221 executions. It has been estimated that the true figure may be even higher. As these are only the figures for official trials, many more accusations must have been made that did not make it to the courts for one reason or another. With a population of only around 70,000, this denotes a higher than average number of accusations. More witches were accused, tried and executed in the Scottish Borders than in any other area of Scotland except Edinburgh and the Lothians. The accusations and trials of witches in Scotland tended to occur in distinct periods, eg 1629, 1649, 1661. While this pattern is also seen in the Borders, there is also a much more consistent level of single cases being brought in the various towns and villages of the region. Between the main periods of high activity, the Borders could always be relied on to be bringing one or two cases when the rest of the country was relatively quiet. The question is why should the Borders have such a high rate of cases for such a low level of population and why, when the apparent threat of witchcraft was dormant in the rest of the country, did the Borders continue to carry out cases? The official records also show that the Borders had very high levels of guilty sentences and executions. At least 63 per cent of those brought to trial in the Borders were executed; the Scottish average was around 55 per cent. These figures do not allow for circumstances where the fate of the accused is unknown due to incomplete or missing records.

The people of the Borders, in common with most of Europe, had an innocent belief in the power of spirits and faeries reaching back to pre-Christian times. This had been, relatively, tolerated in the early days of Christianity. During the medieval period as the church consolidated its power these beliefs start to be seen as part of the Devil's realm. This developed until by the 16th century European theologians started to believe that there were actually people who worshipped the Devil: witches. The Reformation 'proved' to the new Protestant faith that the Devil and his witches with roaming the land. Who else could be responsible for war, famine and plague? The Scottish Kirk, God's Elect, declared war on Auld Nick. But while the Devil was sowing chaos across the land blasting entire communities with the likes of war, he had also sent out his handmaidens to destroy communities from within. To the modern mind, it is obvious that the crimes witches were accused of are impossible. You cannot cause the harvest to fail by casting a spell. However, in the 17th century it was perfectly believable that an individual could cause the harvest to fail. Everyone believed in the existence of God and the Devil and their power. A good Christian could pray to God for help; a witch, aided by the Devil, could cast a spell and cause the harvest to fail.

The Borders was, like many parts of Scotland at the time, an intensely rural area where life for many was lived on the margins and one poor harvest or a cow going sick could result in death from starvation for a family. The line between life and death for many rural poor was a thin one, especially for the young, the old and the already sick. Women caring for the sick or helping as midwives were easy prey for those seeking to blame someone for their own misfortune. As women were, predominantly, in control of the household's food supply, they were also those best placed to curdle a neighbour's milk or spoil a friend's ale. However, rural life was equally harsh across Scotland and the risks of illness and spoiled foods were not particular to the Borders. The reasons behind accusations and the nature of Scottish witch hunts have been extensively documented elsewhere (by Maxwell-Stuart and others) but little, if any, attention has been paid to the particular nature of the witch hunts in the Border lands. Why, with a relatively small and sparse population, did the Borders manifest such a large crop of witches and why did the local presbytery appear to pursue them with such evident vigour? Why, also, did the Borders have trials that ranged from one individual witch to trials involving large numbers of individuals? And why was the Borders home to witches of both genders and all ages?

Was it the geography of the Borders? By its very location, the area had borne the brunt of the frequent wars between Scotland and England. The constant and continual uncertainty and proximity of death and destruction would have played their part in the local psyche. The dark and seemingly uncontrollable forces of war might have become mirrored in many communities by the apparent existence of the equally dark and uncontrollable forces of witchcraft.

Was it the history of the reivers? As Border families had ridden stealing and burning as they went, did witches too creep through the night to steal and ultimately burn? Was it the low number of families involved as ministers, commissioners, sheriffs and baillies? Related by blood or marriage, these men controlled the process from initial investigation, through trial to final execution. And for most an accusation would result in execution.

Or was it something in the mentality of the Borders' Kirk? Were they fearful of the Catholics that still lurked in the north of England? There were uprisings by Catholics in Northumbria as late as 1537 and the Percies and Nevilles and all of their followers were staunch Catholics and previously reivers. Had the Borders clergy been shamed by the religious fervour of the Covenanters in Galloway? The Covenanters had literally fought for their faith, the Borderers had not. Or had the very piety of the Borders become not a blessing from God but a curse by the Devil? Had their Godliness released a plague of witches upon their own Kirk?

I

Belief

Witchcraft in the 17th century

HUMAN CULTURE MOVES slowly and at different speeds for different peoples. It is not tidy and does not fit neatly into nicely labelled time periods. Beliefs and behaviours spill over from one time to another and may mix and evolve over the centuries. This is true for many aspects of human culture, including the spiritual. The Scottish Borders has been populated since around 6500 BC and the evidence suggests that these early Borderers in common with many early societies worshipped various gods or supernatural creatures. The world for these early Borderers could be an unpredictable and frightening place with sudden storms, floods, illnesses and harvest failure. Events outwith human control could mean life or death. In order to make sense of such happenings and in the hope of lessening their occurrence, early Borderers appeased the gods through supplications and prayers. The shadowy gods lurked in many places, most notably water, and a frequent sacrifice was of a metal object cast into water. Metal was precious and water was thought of as a gateway between the human world and the world of the gods. Not everyone could afford to offer a metal sacrifice and food and drink was often offered instead. Magical amulets offered protection from the wrath of certain gods and supplications to others were pleas for good luck.

While various peoples arrived as settlers or invaders, these religious beliefs remained relatively unchanged for several centuries. Around the 5th century AD, the first Christians arrived in the Borders. The new faith took some time to establish itself and, even after Christianity was established, the two beliefs co-existed for some considerable time. Syncretism, the amalgamation or attempted amalgamation of different religions, is seen across human culture and the arrival of Christianity into the Borders was no exception. Blending and cross-fertilisation between the old and the new gave the people enough spiritual solace to ensure ongoing followers for both. The festivals around the winter solstice on 21 December mixed with celebrations of Christ's birth. Equally offerings of thanksgiving at the return of the good weather in spring were subsumed into the Easter celebrations of the resurrected Christ.

Initially the changes were slight, however, as the centuries wound on Christianity became more dominant. As the territories of the old Roman Empire were Christianised, so too were the members of the ruling orders and those engaged in trade. But although Christianised, many people retained traditions and practices from their pre-Christian past. Initially the early Christian church accepted many of these traditions but, as the church strengthened and grew, its tolerance diminished.

There were three main points of contention: a single Christian God rather than several pagan gods; the Christian separation of good and evil into two different entities, while the old beliefs had contented itself with a duality within their gods; and one single male God within Christianity rather than the female as well as male gods of before. In addition, the clarity that was self-evident to Christians was confusing to pagans. Christianity was clear: there was one God, who was good and male and there was one evil Devil. But this surface simplicity quickly gave way as it was revealed that the one God was also Christ the son and the Holy Spirit. And why had the one good god, who had created all, created an evil Devil? To the old believers, this sounded curiously like multiple gods who were both good and evil and what was the Virgin Mary if not a female god?

Theological arguments aside, the day-to-day business of life was little altered by the new religion. Appeasing the gods for a good harvest mutated into the priest blessing the fields at spring sowing. Thanking the gods for an abundant crop became the harvest thanksgiving festival at the local church. In rural areas, a reasonable, if unspoken, accommodation was reached at which a priest might turn a blind eye to certain superstitions, as the old beliefs were now called, as long as there was a genuine belief in God. A simple faith was accepted, albeit one which did not bear too much scrutiny.

This relatively peaceful co-existence could not last forever. By the 16th century, an unthinking, non-questioning belief was no longer good enough and the Reformation jolted rural areas out of their religious torpor. The new focus on personal salvation and the word of the Bible removed many of the ritual elements of Catholicism; those very elements which had held reassuring remnants of the old folk beliefs. Correct theology was no longer the preserve of priests and bishops but was to be understood by all. As the Reformation progressed in Scotland, more and more people converted to the Protestant faith. However, for many, Protestant theology was ill-equipped to deal with the complexities of everyday life and they simply brought their pagan beliefs with them.

Those beliefs were expressed in many ways but were dominated by death. Death was a common visitor in the many rural areas of Scotland – as indeed it was for most of rural Europe – including the Borders, through illness, wars or famine. The old beliefs had offered a method of articulating fears and dealing with the spirits of the dead. This had been continued by the Catholic faith with its masses for the dead. The ways of the old gods or the new God could not be understood but religious ritual could provide comfort. The new Protestant faith singularly failed to provide a similar method of comfort. The new faith expected individuals to think about their relationship with God. Were they saved or damned? Who could know for certain? Individuals were further expected to think about their faith at all times. But thinking about religion did not alter the reality of rural life. The harvest still failed, illness still came, family members still died. And everyone knew that the spirits of the dead had to be appeased to protect the living from their anger and to ease their passage into the other world. The lack of understanding by the Protestant clergy of this basic underlying belief would prove disastrous. Ghosts, spirits and apparitions were a fact of life and if the new faith would not or could not cater to this belief, and the Catholic faith was branded diabolical, then the people would simply reach back to the old days for succour; Halloween would give them that aid. Condemned outright by the Kirk, Halloween would prove to be a tenacious relic of the pagan beliefs.

Try as it might, the Christian church could not shake the festival of Halloween. But what it could and did do was to demonise those who participated. The lack of understanding from the Kirk and the intransigence of ordinary people made any accommodation impossible. As far as the Christian fathers were concerned, Halloween with its necromancy was simple Devil worship by another name. For rural people, however, while they retained their belief in God and attended the Kirk on a Sunday, the folk beliefs in talking to spirits and ghosts remained. The local minster might talk of the riches of heaven in the life to come but a spinning apple might give some forewarning of a bad winter in the here and now.

The Kirk believed that witches had renounced their Christianity and made a pact or covenant with the Devil. The people, however, did not think in such formalised terms. Carrying a lucky amulet was not seen by Borders villagers as anti-Christian, but merely a normal activity, albeit a cultural throwback to the old ways. They were able to accommodate their Christianity and their superstition; the Kirk was not.

What had previously been tolerated, to a degree, by the Catholic Church was anathema to the new Presbyterian Kirk. Practices that had been innocently pursued were now castigated and given a diabolical basis. In the early days of the Kirk's witch hunts, people confessed, not because they were mad or confused or even tortured. They confessed that, yes, they had left an offering to the man with the black hat or had looked in water to find stolen property. These were the common activities of most people. While some were, no doubt, witches in the eyes of both themselves and their neighbours, the vast majority were just ordinary people with superstitious beliefs. Their confessions were true. It was simply that what was a normal procedure for them and had been practised for generations had become an act of evil to the Kirk.

While many did confess to making a pact with the Devil, care must be taken over this. Some of those who confessed to making a covenant with Auld Nick, as the Devil was occasionally known, did genuinely believe that they had met him. However, it must be remembered that the fervent beliefs of the interrogators led them to try to discover a diabolic element to witchcraft and frame their questioning accordingly. This was not a case of manipulating the questions to get the answers they wanted but a matter of stressing the questions that they felt would allow them to get at the real truth of the matter: the Devil and his works. When witches said they made a covenant, this was not Devil worship as a cult – an alternative religious belief to Christianity – it was more a pact between one person and Auld Nick. The old gods had been creatures with whom an individual could bargain; I will sacrifice in order for you to ensure a good harvest or, if you give me a male child, I will make a sacrifice in your honour. However, the Protestant Reformation had introduced a new aspect of personal responsibility and a covenant with God. Witches were damned, therefore, for their choice of the Devil over God and their method of interaction with him which mocked the covenant with the Presbyterian God.

Witches' confessions were not the fevered tales of Gothic horror. They were often much more mundane, coming from sometimes lonely, sometimes poor people, who believed they had met the Devil and that he had made them promises of power over their enemies or ample food for the winter. They made a covenant with the Devil and got revenge on those who had slighted them. A neighbour, who years previously had refused to help, would lose a cow. An unpaid debt would see ale soured. There was little if any flying around on broomsticks or turning your neighbour into a toad. These were everyday matters: causing the milk of a neighbour's cow to dry up, spoiling ale, raising a storm to ruin crops. But everyday matters though they were, they were also matters of life and death. For the rural poor of the Borders life was a constant struggle and many lived on the precarious edge between survival and destitution. If a rich farmer's crops were ruined by a storm, he might be able to buy in food to feed his family. If a poor tenant farmer lost his crops, his family faced several lean weeks. For a farm labourer, a crop failure would mean no wages and possible starvation.

It was women who were responsible for maintaining the home. Ensuring the family was fed was female work; churning milk to make butter, brewing ale for the men to drink. If a cow went dry or the ale soured, it was the women who were to blame. What could start as a neighbourhood quarrel would all too soon descend into darker waters. Cursing a neighbour's crops or kye (cattle) or wishing illness on a horse or even a child as revenge for an apparent injury with little risk of capture was too easy a lure to reject. It is rare in any of the trial records to hear of witches being promised or seeking after great riches. These were years of food shortages and war. You were much more likely to survive through the winter with your kye alive and healthy than with a hoard of gold beneath your bed.

In the vast majority of cases, the accusations that arose from such household quarrels and the curses of the injured party were considered witchcraft by the Kirk. In some of the cases, albeit the minority, the injured parties believed themselves to be witches. While most 17th century Scots were merely superstitious, continuing the ritual of the old ways while attending the Kirk on a Sunday, there were those who were known as and believed themselves to be witches. Sought out by their neighbours in times of trouble, they used their craft in ways that threatened Kirk authority. Like devout members of the Kirk, witches believed in a supernatural being who would reward you for worshipping him and following his code of behaviour. Unfortunately for the witches, their supernatural being was unacceptable to the powers that be.

The religious and superstitious beliefs of most people in the 17th century were no different from those held in the 16th century, or for that matter the beliefs that would prevail in the 18th century. What was to prove fatal was the inability of the Kirk to accept any deviation from the prescribed dogma of the day, and the inability of ordinary folk to dissemble. It has been suggested that one of the reasons why the nobility were rarely arrested for witchcraft was not that they did not believe in witches or indulge in witchcraft; it was rather that they were better liars and better able to hide their superstitious beliefs behind a façade of Christian respectability than the folk of the Borders.

It is likely that of all those arrested for witchcraft some would, no doubt, have described themselves as witches. The vast majority were trying to survive in a harsh world as best they could and were innocent of the charges brought against them.

2

History

The Borders in the 17th century

THE HUNT FOR witches in the Scottish Borders appears to have been characterised by levels of religious zeal seldom seen elsewhere. But this religious zeal should not be thought of as an excuse to attack women (although women were predominantly accused) nor should it be thought of as an organisation out of control and drunk on power, although again there were instances of individuals abusing their position of authority. Both ideals are somewhat anachronistic. The religious zeal with which the Borders Kirk pursued witches was based on a genuine fear: fear of the Devil. As the century progressed, the Borders Kirk came to believe themselves to be under attack by the Devil himself. Their reasoning was threefold.

Firstly, the Kirk believed that they were God's Elect. A central part of Jean Calvin's theology taught that all events had been preordained by God; that He had willed eternal damnation for some and salvation for others. Book III of Calvin's Institutes of the Christian Religion detailed 'the eternal election, by which God has predestinated some to salvation, and others to destruction'.[2] As religious Scots that had chosen Calvinism, the members of the Kirk believed they had already been elected by God for salvation. However, this conviction led to a degree of unease as no one could know for sure if they were saved. Proof would be needed. This then led to the second element of their argument. If they were indeed God's Elect then they would be targeted by the Devil for attack. He had no reason to attack his own but would surely turn his malice towards the most godly, God's Elect. The Kirk's very godliness, therefore, made it a target. And just as they (the Kirk) covered all of Scotland, so the Devil would unleash a horde of his followers (witches) across the land to attack them.

As the 17th century developed, this became something of a self-fulfilling prophecy. The more godly the Kirk, the greater the number of attacks by witches and so, perversely, the Kirk became drawn into denouncing more and more witches. This prophecy was based on a belief in the Kirk's status as God's Elect and a genuine fear of the Devil and his works, it was 'proved', in the mind of the clergy, by the chaos of the civil and religious wars of the century and the repeated occurrences of plague and famine. This third element of the Kirk's reasoning had a particular resonance in the Scottish Borders as its geographical location resulted in a perfect storm of events and circumstances. The Borders became the site of repeated battles as Royalists, parliamentarians and Covenanters fought for control. Even when the various armies were not fighting in the Borders, they wrought destruction as they passed through on the road to Edinburgh or Newcastle. Armies at that time lived off the land and a passing troop of soldiers could strip a community of all of its food stores in a day. Those who resisted were assaulted, as were any young women who caught the eye of the soldiers. In addition, the Borders Kirk was conscious of the proximity of the Catholics in the north of England who had resolutely failed to abandon the old, and now very suspect, faith. Had not Knox himself preached that Catholics were in league with the Devil? And finally, disease and harvest failure visited the Borders on multiple occasions over the century, devastating many communities. The four horsemen of pestilence, war, famine and death rode across the land, or so it seemed. Beleaguered as the Borders Kirk felt themselves to be, they developed something of a siege mentality. Under attack by war, devastated by harvest failures and plague, threatened by Catholics, the religious fervour of the Borders Kirk quickly became hysteria as the events of the century pushed it from the spiritual ecstasy of being God's Elect into the delusional frenzy of a church under attack by Auld Nick himself.

To put the Scottish witch hunts into some perspective, the level of witchcraft trials in Scotland per head of population was one of the highest in Europe and ten times the rate in neighbouring England. The rate of trials and executions in the Borders was the second highest in Scotland despite the area having a relatively low population.

The 17th century saw Scotland still reeling from the effects of the great religious wars of the Reformation and Counter-Reformation. The Reformation that had swept most of northern Europe arrived in Scotland in various forms in the early 16th century. The beliefs of Luther and Calvin and their criticisms of the church were vigorously debated by many including John Knox of Haddington. One of Calvin's most fervent followers, Knox's influence on the direction of the new church was pivotal. After narrowly escaping arrest alongside his mentor, George Wishart, Knox was captured by the French before being released when he took refuge in England and served as royal Chaplain to Edward VI. After the accession of Catholic Mary Tudor to the English throne, Knox resigned his post and fled to Geneva where he met Calvin. On meeting Calvin, Knox asked a series of revealing questions. Could a minor rule by divine right? Should people obey ungodly or idolatrous rulers? What party should godly persons follow if they resisted an idolatrous ruler? And could a female rule and transfer sovereignty to her husband? These questions were highly political and related, in the main, to the rule of Mary Tudor. Although Calvin, ever the politician, gave somewhat cautious answers to Knox, the issue of women and power would remain integral to much of Knox's thinking for the rest of his life. Knox spent his time on the continent thinking and reading on Calvin's work and reworking the theology into his own world view and understanding of God. This became a worldview comprising rigid certainty in the correctness of Calvinist Protestantism and an unbending opposition to anything which appeared to transgress that belief.

The Protestant Reformation in Scotland was Calvinist in nature and became Knoxian in execution. In 1557, the Lords of the Congregation drew up their covenant to 'maintain, set forth, and establish the most blessed Word of God and his Congregation.'[3] When the Scottish Parliament convened on 1 August 1560, they set up a 'committee of the articles' consisting of Knox and five other ministers. This committee was to draw up a new confession of faith. Knox presented his recommendations in the Scots Confession which called for a condemnation of papal authority, a restoration of early Church discipline and a redistribution of Church wealth to the ministry and the poor. Parliament approved the Scots Confession of Faith and passed three Acts that destroyed the old Catholic faith in Scotland: the abolition of the jurisdiction of the Pope in Scotland; the condemnation of all doctrine and practice contrary to the reformed faith; and the outlawing of the celebration of mass in Scotland. On paper, at least, the Reformation was established in Scotland. In practice, it would prove to be a somewhat different matter.

Knox and his colleagues were asked to undertake the organisation of the reformed church. After several months of work, they produced the *Book of Discipline*[4] which set out the organisation of the new church. *The Second Book of Discipline* was published in 1578 after the death of Knox and the abdication of Mary, Queen of Scots. It was a reiteration of Knox's values and firmly established Presbyterianism in Scotland. The new church organisation set out in the *Book of Discipline* allowed each Kirk a relatively large degree of autonomy. Each congregation could choose or reject their own minister; although, once chosen, they could not fire him. Each parish was to be self-supporting and bishops were replaced by a group of 10–12 'superintendents'. The new Kirk was to be financed from the patrimony of the Roman Catholic Church. This proved somewhat contentious as much of the land that had been confiscated from the Catholic Church had been given to members of the nobility who were loathe to relinquish it – especially those who still retained a belief in the old faith. A further measure which rankled with the nobility was for certain areas of the law to be placed under ecclesiastical authority, diminishing, in the eyes of those nobles, their own power. The removal of the power of Rome had been welcomed by much of the nobility, no matter their faith, as it was seen as an opportunity to consolidate and in some cases extend their own authority. The increased autonomy of the Kirk with its superintendents was therefore an undesirable element in the new reformed Scotland and one that was to be resisted.

The Parliament did not, in fact, approve the *Book of Discipline* due, in part, to financial reasons and stiff opposition from many nobles, but also due to the imminent arrival of Mary, Queen of Scots, which put all matters, especially religious, on hold. However, the basic structure of the new Kirk had been established. The autonomy given to individual Kirks would prove a dangerous element later when witchcraft accusations were made. With no need for ministers to seek advice or approval from a higher church authority, the Borders Kirk had no restraining voice to caution.

A second element that would exert a strong influence on the 17th Scottish Kirk was Knox's attitude towards both witches and women, which had continued to develop since his initial struggles with Mary, Queen of Scots. His famous pamphlet, *The First Blast of the Trumpet against the Monstrous Regiment of Women*[5], may have been aimed at powerful women such as Mary, Queen of Scots and Mary Tudor of England but, like all such documents, once printed it took on a life of its own and percolated into the psyche of many. Its central message – that power was not a state natural to women, that women would always seek power over men and that women who sought power were to be feared – struck a chord with many across Scotland, especially those in the Kirk and the nobility. The Reformation had several unintended consequences, one of which was that educated noble women started to read their Bibles. Without the need of a male priest to explain or intercede for them with God, some of these women questioned their need for men in their day-to-day lives. Previous beliefs about women and their place in society were now questioned, albeit by a very small minority. The subservient role of women touched on another issue of great import to the Kirk: the matter of authority. Desperate to put the genie back in the bottle, Knox wrote his *First Blast of the Trumpet*, conflated any and all women with witches or potential witches and preached hellfire and damnation to any who questioned the natural order of men as superior to women. For the average Scot who still could not even read their Bible, Knox's powerful sermons, which were repeated from many pulpits, won the day. Any fledgling notions of female emancipation were squashed and the belief that no woman was ever to be truly trusted was given religious legitimacy. This message, in combination with other factors, would play its part in the preponderance of female witchcraft victims brought to trial in Scotland.

As the Scots were Godly, so the Devil would attack us. As he needed servants, so he would use untrustworthy women. So, for Knox, witches were, as handmaidens of the Devil, quite simply the enemy of God and his people. The rooting out and execution of witches was, therefore, nothing less than war.

> For all those that would draw us from God (be they Kings or Quenes) being of the Devil's nature, are enemyis unto God, and therefore will God that in such cases we declare ourselves enemyis unto them.[6]

The understanding that witches were the servants of the Devil accorded perfectly with Knox's view of women as creatures subservient to men. The alternative view that witches were independent beings with a degree of power was simply unthinkable. This insistence by Knox on a link between witchcraft and the Devil merely served to give a solid base to the Kirk's later understanding and treatment of witches; a base that lasted until the end of the 17th century. The political and religious upheavals of the 17th century all centred on the matter of authority. The Reformation had fought long and hard to rid society of the 'false authority' of popes and priests. True authority came solely from the word of God and the Kirk was the true keeper of that word. For women to use the word of God in charms to ensure a fertile marriage bed or a good harvest was blasphemous; God was not at the beck and call of women. And, consequently, if their actions did not come from God, there was only one other place from which they could emanate: the Devil.

One of the main changes in the organisation of the Kirk was that candidates for the ministry were to be examined as to their suitability for the post of minister and then be elected by the local congregation. The congregation would be led by a committee of elders. Most ministers would be elected from the committee. Power would, therefore, come to be concentrated in the hands of those elders. The Kirk was also to engage in education which was to be established at all levels from village school to university and while this would lead to increased literacy among the Scots, it was mainly used at a local level to teach communities the correct moral code by which to live. This was determined by the elders who also policed the morals of their congregations and passed judgement on those found to be in breach of the code. And a new moral code was desperately needed. Despite the Reformation, belief in many of the tenets of the Catholic faith, and even older superstitions, had stubbornly remained a feature of Scottish life and would prove to be a thorny issue for many years for the Kirk.

The Christian faith had, in its early days in Scotland and elsewhere, absorbed many pagan customs and practices. Early church missionaries had understood that in the matter of local customs a degree of leniency was a better method of gaining converts than coercion. But that had been the old Catholic way and Scotland was now a Calvinist nation where superstitions were viewed at best as the remains of the old disgraced faith and at worst as leading to the Devil, and as such had to be stamped out. Where before belief in kelpies and lucky charms had been part and parcel of life, they were now viewed with increasing suspicion and disapproval. Tellingly, in the Highlands and Islands of Scotland where Catholicism lingered longest, superstitious beliefs were also treated with greater leniency. This was also the area of Scotland with the fewest witchcraft trials.

Auld Nick would prove a tenacious foe throughout the 17th century as he sought to undermine the new faith. When old Queen Elizabeth of England finally died in 1603 and James VI of Scotland finally gained the English throne, few would have predicted that this would be the start of a turbulent century for both countries. It was said, by more than a few, that James was quite glad to be quit of Scotland for her richer southern neighbour and it is true that England was, by comparison with Scotland, a much richer nation. But there were also not a few that said James was equally glad to be leaving a country where only 13 years previously a coven of witches had tried to drown him and his Danish bride at North Berwick.

Whatever the truth of the matter, James was to return to his native land only once between 1603 and his death in 1625. With no King in the land, the rule of Scotland was left in the hands of the Parliament and the Kirk. James, busy with his new court life in London, diplomatically left the religion of the Scots to the Scots, with the Presbyterian Kirk initially managing a reasonable co-existence with other faiths and forms.

While the religious situation in Scotland remained relatively calm, trouble was brewing on the continent as various European powers consolidated their religious affiliations while suspiciously eyeing up the position of their neighbours. These tensions eventually exploded in 1618 when war broke out. The conflict would last until 1648 and became known as the Thirty Years' War.[7] The Peace of Augsburg of 1555 had previously established the principle of *Cuius regio, eius religio*, which allowed Princes within the Holy Roman Empire to choose the religion of their region. However, although the peace gave those who objected to their Prince's choice a period of time in which to leave the Prince's land, it had not fully resolved the underlying tensions which had been exacerbated by the spread of Protestantism across the German states. The war of 1618 soon enveloped almost all the European powers as religious and political issues intertwined. While Protestant and Catholic states fought each other over religion, the Bourbon and Habsburg dynasties also fought for political domination. Lesser states saw potential for increasing their territory, while not a few settled for interfering in their neighbours' lands when it suited them.

King James was a shrewd statesman and managed to steer Britain on a precarious political course between the competing interests in Europe. Never declaring war himself, James confined his interest to supplying men (often clandestinely as mercenaries), arms and money to those with whom he could do business within the various Protestant nations. Conscious of the combination of political and religious elements within the conflict, James sought to protect the trading interest of Britain first and foremost while influencing much behind the scenes. However, although this politically astute policy won James much support and respect among London merchants, it did little to calm the fears of the Borders Kirk who saw the Devil visiting war and destruction across Europe. Tall tales of atrocities inflicted on Protestants by rabid Catholic troops did little to quell their fears. And the Kirk had other proof that the Devil was abroad in the world. From 1600 onwards, lowland Scotland suffered disease, famine, war and death while surrounded by wild Catholics; the mentality of the Borders Kirk was firmly set.

It was at this inopportune moment that James died and his son, Charles I, ascended to the throne. Charles was a very different man from his father. His belief in the Divine Right of Kings was absolute. He was a holy anointed King who ruled by the Grace of God and he was determined to make his mark. Unfortunately, this belief rendered him incapable of the degree of subtlety with which had father had reigned. He lacked his father's political nous and in the case of Scotland, he also appears to have had a lack of understanding of how his northern nation functioned and did not seem eager to learn. James had been destined to unify the crowns of the old enemies of Scotland and England. He had also wished for a uniformity of faith over his two nations but, given his understanding of the nature of the Kirk in Scotland, he had been diplomatic enough to lay that desire aside. Charles, realising the legacy he had inherited from his father, also wished for a uniformity of faith over his entire Kingdom. If James had united the crowns, Charles would unify the faith. The kingdom had one King and would have one faith; unfortunately for Scotland, Charles favoured the Episcopal faith over the Calvinist Presbyterian. This was partly a matter of familiarity, as the Episcopal faith was the faith of the court in London, and partly a matter of political necessity. The imposition of a single faith on the population would be easier if the nobility were in agreement. The nobility in Scotland were fewer in number, further in distance and lesser in influence than their English counterparts. The Presbyterian faith, quite simply, had fewer supporters in the London court.

But there was another reason Charles favoured the Episcopal Faith. Charles' belief in the Divine Right of Kings did not sit well with many in England. Voices were increasingly clamouring for a greater say in the running of their country; a strengthened role for parliament. This was anathema to Charles, whose initial response to such impertinence was, somewhat ill-advisedly, to ignore it. However, the Episcopal faith with its hierarchy of bishops and with the King at its head mirrored and supported Charles' image of his rule. The Presbyterian Kirk with its elders who had the power to elect ministers was uncomfortably parliamentarian in its form.

By 1629, barely four years into his reign, Charles was governing without the Parliament in London. He failed to grasp the growing tensions within his rule and, when these did become clear to him, his solution was simple and devastating: he dissolved Parliament. With no opposition to challenge him and few honest counsellors to advise him, he started on his plans to reform the religion of his Kingdom.

But it was a kingdom that he barely knew outside London and the south-east of England. In 1637, Charles, failing to understand the place of the Kirk in Scottish society, decided, with the help of the Archbishop of Canterbury, William Laud, to impose the Anglican hierarchy and full liturgy on the Church in Scotland. In 1638, the Scots, understanding completely what the King was attempting to do, rioted and created the National Covenant. His actions had reignited the fears of the old Covenanters. Lord Warriston, Archibald Johnston, worked with the senior Scottish theologian, Alexander Henderson, to revive the National Covenant of 1581. The new Covenant was adopted and signed in Greyfriars Kirkyard in Edinburgh in 1638 and copies of the Covenant were distributed throughout the country for signing. The Covenanters then raised an army to defend the Scots religion and resist the imposition of any reforms by Charles I. (In 1640, the Covenant was adopted by the Scottish Parliament and its subscription was made compulsory for all citizens.)

By 1639, the Covenanters had taken control of several Scottish towns including Edinburgh and Stirling, while the General Assembly of the Kirk abolished the previously tolerated episcopal form of worship. Charles, outraged by the Scottish upstarts, declared war on the Covenanters. His previous decision to rule without Parliament then thwarted his attempts to deal with the Scots. He lacked the funds to pay for an army and he was forced to recall Parliament to ask for money. The English parliamentarians, however, were reluctant to raise money for a conflict that was of little interest to them and had been, in their opinion, generated by a King who had previously ignored them. Charles was also stymied by the lack of experience of many of his commanders and the ferocity of resistance shown by the Covenanters. In 1639, the King managed to broker an uneasy truce. Failing again to understand the mood of the Scots, Charles ignored the unspoken but implicit conditions of the truce, to abandon attempts to impose episcopacy in Scotland, and continued with his reforms as before while also raising more funds to train an army against the unruly Covenanters who had dared to challenge his royal authority.

By 1640, the Covenanters, angered by the King's duplicity, were on the march down through the Borders to Newcastle. Charles summoned the Parliament in London for assistance but was disappointed by another lukewarm response to his request and shocked by a list of unprecedented demands from the parliamentarians in exchange for their support. The Covenanters were now clear in their aim; if the King wanted one faith across the kingdom so did they: Presbyterian Calvinism. The Royalists and parliamentarians, at something of a stalemate, both started to court the Covenanters, who eventually made an alliance, the Solemn League and Covenant of 1643, with the parliamentarians. This Covenant pledged the Scottish army to fight for the English parliamentary cause in return for religious support. Borders men would be called to serve in the army. While the Covenanters believed the Solemn League and Covenant committed the parliamentarians to the establishment of a national Presbyterian church both north and south of the border, the parliamentarians did not favour Presbyterian rule. They viewed the Covenant merely as a convenient means to an end; to clip the King's wings.

The wars would rage over the whole of the United Kingdom and the Borders was no exception. In 1645, Royalist troops led by Montrose met with the Covenanters led by Leslie at Philiphaugh near Selkirk. The Covenanters defeated the Royalist army and Montrose fled the field. Many of the Irish foot soldiers, who had fought for Montrose, surrendered under the promise of quarter. In military terms, to give quarter meant that a victor was willing to take care of prisoners. To house and feed a prisoner, one would give them quarters and quarter them, that is food and shelter. Undaunted by this pledge of honour, several Kirk ministers urged the Covenanters to put the Irish to the sword. This slaughter included the camp followers which comprised around 300 women and children.

In 1646, Charles surrendered to the Scottish army at Newark. Unable to reach any agreement with the King, the army handed him over to the English. Politics continued to ebb and flow and in 1648 the Covenanters, disappointed by the English parliamentarians' lack of support for a unified Presbyterian faith, fought for Charles against Cromwell. The Covenanters invaded England on the King's behalf, riling the English population who saw a King making war on his own people alongside 'foreign' Scottish troops. However, the parliamentarian troops were well disciplined, well-armed and larger in number. In 1651, the Scots army was defeated at Worcester and, in 1652, Scotland came under English parliamentary rule. Lowland Scotland, including the Borders, was occupied by the English army and Cromwell imposed the Commonwealth on the Scots which broke the parliamentary power of the Covenanters.

For eight years, although chafing under English rule, Scotland, and the Borders, remained free from battles. During this time, the Scottish harvest remained good and no serious outbreaks of plague were recorded. While this freedom from war, disease and starvation should have been seen as a respite from the Devil and his works, it was undermined by one momentous event that was unthinkable to almost all, even as it was happening; the execution of the King by Parliament. Despite all his faults (and they were many), not least the attempt to impose episcopacy on the Scots, to execute the King was the world turned upside down in the eyes of the Kirk. A King could be mad or even bad, but he was still King. Not even royals could execute each other with impunity. The execution of Mary, Queen of Scots by her cousin Elizabeth of England had been condemned by almost every monarch and prince in Europe, including those of the Protestant faith, many fearing the precedent which this set. This latest execution of a Prince of the blood royal was an outrage.

The Parliament in Scotland proclaimed Charles' son King Charles II of Great Britain and Ireland; the Parliament in England declared all such proclamations unlawful. As far as the Kirk was concerned, for common men to execute a Prince of the blood royal disrupted the natural order. If a King could be executed then anything was possible, the normal rule no longer pertained and this must surely herald the rule of the Devil. Then barely eight years later, the same parliamentarians who had fought a war, executed a King and declared a republic approached Charles' son and asked him to return to the throne. Britain would become a monarchy again.

Charles was restored to the throne in 1660. Personally, he was tolerant in matters of religion but in the first years of the Restoration with his position not yet consolidated, he signed the Clarendon Code which bolstered the Church of England at the expense of other faiths in England, most notably Catholics. The Code included several measures which alarmed the Scottish Kirk. It formally rejected the

Solemn League and Covenant of 1643 which resulted in the exclusion of non-conformists from public office. The Act of Uniformity was imposed which made the use of the Book of Common Prayer compulsory in religious service, and the Conventicle Act forbade conventicles (meetings of unauthorised worship) of more than five people who were not members of the same household. The Kirk was in uproar. The Restoration of the monarchy had pointed to the return of the natural order and evidenced that the Devil, for all his tricks and hordes of witches, was losing his grip on the people. And yet this monarch seemed prepared to undermine the Presbyterian nature of the Kirk in Scotland even to the point of imposing episcopacy again. Several hundred Presbyterian ministers took to the hills and preached in open conventicles. Attendance at conventicles was declared a capital offence and, by 1666, armed Covenanters and Government troops were once again doing battle across the Scottish countryside. The Covenanters were most numerous in the Galloway area and the Borders Kirk watched as the Devil roamed the land once more dispensing death and destruction, while even clergymen were hunted down by their erstwhile colleagues. As if that were not enough to terrify the beleaguered members of the Kirk, the Great Fire of London broke out in September of the same year. Rumours about the fire ran wild, with many blaming Catholics. A Frenchman, Robert Hubert, was hanged after confessing to having started the fire while acting as an agent of the Pope. It was later proved that he had not even arrived in London until after the fire had started but that news barely reached the – by now almost hysterical – clergy in the Borders.

The situation with the Covenanters was exacerbated when the Government decided to bring in Highland troops to quell what they saw as a rebellion. Unfortunately, the use of highlanders inflamed the fears of the Borders Kirk who saw these 'Catholics' as doing the handiwork of the Devil. The atrocities committed by these troops, some real, some imagined, added to the terror. For the Covenanters and their supporters, this was a matter of deeply held religious belief. For the government, it was a matter of public rebellion which, as everyone knew, could lead to revolution – and no one wanted a return to that. Unfortunately, in late 1678, many of the Covenanters started to harden their stance. Most Covenanters had previously professed at least an outward loyalty to the King. However, this was slowly changing, due in part to the repressive measures imposed against them, but also to their fears over the royal succession. Charles showed no signs of producing a legitimate heir and next in line to the throne was his brother James, a suspected Catholic. The Covenanters rose again and this time saw more people joining, most notably from Lanarkshire, Ayrshire and Glasgow and again with few from the Borders. The increased numbers caused dissent among the Covenanters as to their demands. Less time was spent preparing for fighting and more on bickering over styles and forms of worship and authority. As a result, they were defeated at the battle of Bothwell brig near Glasgow in 1679 by Government troops. Despite this defeat, in 1680, under the leadership of the Reverend Richard Cameron, the Covenanters publicly renounced their allegiance to Charles and denounced James as a papist. Known as the Sanquhar Declaration, this was met with field executions as the government ruthlessly suppressed the rebels. Members of the Kirk across much of Scotland, even those loyal to the King, started to raise their voices against the reprisals. For whatever reason, the Borders Kirk remained silent.

In 1685, the worst fears of the Covenanters were realised when Charles died and his brother James succeeded to the throne. The Kirk waited to see how the new 'Catholic' King would reign: would the Covenanters rise again? In order to break the Covenanters once and for all, James issued a series of *Letters of Indulgence* which allowed such 'ousted ministers as had lived peaceably and orderly to return to their livings'. Many Covenanters, exhausted by the previous battles, returned to their parishes including most of the few Borders ministers that had taken a stance. For most ministers in the west, however, this was a betrayal of the Covenant and they refused to return, became more zealous in their beliefs and looked down on those who had returned to their parishes. James, however, had problems of his own to deal with in London, where he was unpopular with the Protestant majority at Court.

In 1689, James fathered a son and the English Protestants were faced with the threat of the establishment of a Catholic dynasty.

In 1690, several English Protestant lords approached James' daughter Mary, a Protestant, and her husband William, and offered them the throne. The Glorious Revolution saw Scotland divided as many supported the ousted King, most of whom were Episcopalian. In contrast, the Presbyterians supported Protestant William and Mary. Seeking peace in the kingdom and recognising the different nature of faith north of the Border, in 1690 the new monarchs formally recognised the Presbyterian form of government for the Kirk. Once on the throne, however, William failed to revive the binding obligation of the National Covenant (1638) and the Solemn League and Covenant (1643). For some Covenanters, this was a bitter disappointment and they considered William an 'uncovenanted' King as he was head of the Church of England which was an Episcopal church. This view was held most strongly in the south-west with around 1,000 people denouncing William's failure to maintain the Covenant. This became a point of contention for some as they felt that the Church of Scotland without the Covenant in its foundation had been 'usurped'. None of the clergy in the Borders adopted this opinion and in fact most avoided the discussion.

While it might be thought that the Covenanters would be welcomed by the Borders Kirk – and they were, up to a point – they also posed a problem. Despite claims that they were God's Elect and that this was why they were attacked by the Devil and his hellish witches, the Borders had produced few Covenanters. The Borders clergy might preach about the defence of the faith but when called to arms, it had been Galloway and the west that produced the greatest numbers of Covenanters willing to actually lay down their lives to defend the true faith. Even the great Covenanter army of Sir David Leslie that had won the battle of Philiphaugh near Selkirk comprised few Borderers. The influence of the Borders Kirk had been confined to urging Leslie's troops to slaughter those Royalist troops that surrendered and their camp followers; an action that was regarded as an un-Christian act at the time.

It has been estimated that some 18,000 Covenanters were killed between 1661 and 1680. Of those, the majority came from the south-west of Scotland. Rightly or wrongly they had literally fought for the defence of their faith. Although they received some support from the Borders, it was considerably less than might be expected in view of the geographical location of the Borders and the vehemence with which the Borders Kirk claimed to be God's Elect. This apparent and public lack of support left the Borders Kirk with an unspoken but very real sense of shame and guilt.

In all these political machinations, the Borders of the 17th century was, like most of Scotland at that time, a sparsely populated rural society. Even without wars and religious upheaval, rural societies in Scotland had two great fears: plague and famine. Both could spell disaster for communities large and small and in the 17th century would stalk the rural families of the Borders again and again. Between 1600 and 1700, famine and plague occurred six times each. On three particularly harsh occasions, both occurred in the same year. In each visitation, the Borders would find the authorities in Edinburgh at best incompetent and at worst complicit in exacerbating the circumstances.

The century started with an outbreak of plague; it was not auspicious. Plague had first arrived in Scotland in 1350, when approximately one third of the population died. It had returned periodically over the years, appearing from nowhere and killing without mercy. It remained to most a terrifying spectre. The response to the cry of plague, therefore, was devastating and affected everyone. Whatever the specific illness and its nature, in an era before any form of antibiotics, death was almost a certainty. Death could be mercifully quick or long and lingering. For the rural poor of the Borders, one member of the family with plague could ring the death knell for an entire family. Most households lived in two room cottages with one main room for eating and one for sleeping; there was simply no space in which to isolate a sick member of the family. Bedding and eating utensils were shared and thus increased the spread of disease. While most disease and illness were relatively well recognised, if not understood, plague was different. The indiscriminate nature of its proliferation set it apart from other diseases, and thus it came to be thought of as either a punishment from God for sin or a visitation from Auld Nick. For the Kirk in the Borders, the former was unthinkable while the latter was perfectly plausible.

The 1600 episode of plague was followed by another in 1607. And just as before, the old, the young and those already ill or weak died. But plague also brought less obvious problems. The great plague that had swept across Europe had overwhelmed great cities, swept away villages and perplexed the doctors of its day. Some lessons were learnt. The city authorities in Dubrovnik had decreed that visitors and ships must be isolated for 40 days before entering their city to see if any passengers developed symptoms of the plague. Venetian traders named this *quaranta giorni*. An excellent disease prevention method, it was to be adopted by many authorities, including Scottish, in the following centuries. However, its use could also prove problematic.

When plague was declared in the Borders, almost all trade and communication came to a standstill as quarantine was imposed. This was imposed locally either officially or unofficially, as many refused to buy from or sell to those suspected of having the plague. For wealthy farmers with food stores or some savings, restrictions on trade were irksome but could be borne until the plague passed. For the average Borderer, however, without such resources, the inability to buy or sell goods could mean several weeks of eating barely a subsistence diet. While these periods of semi-starvation might not mean death, they left many in a weakened state and susceptible to other illnesses or injuries. And, of course, if the period of quarantine was prolonged then death from starvation could occur. Quarantine could also be imposed by the authorities in Edinburgh who could place restrictions on the movements of people and goods across the entire Borders. This was widely resented, partly as it placed restrictions on such a large area but also as the lack of knowledge and understanding of the Borders by the Edinburgh authorities resulted in restrictions that were nonsensical. The town of Selkirk had occasion to plead with Edinburgh to lift restrictions placed upon it by authorities convinced that the town lay across the border in England. The appearance of plague on two occasions within seven years gave rise to a mini panic. Some perfectly healthy individuals and communities suspected of having the plague were shunned and some individuals starved to death in their own homes, unable to leave for fear of their neighbours. There was nothing for it but to sit it out. Some survived, many did not.

And then, in 1623, famine struck. Famine can occur for several reasons: climatic, economic, social, political or a combination of factors. The 17th century was a period of cooler temperatures across northern Europe. This reduced the growing season across Scotland and increased pressure on existing farming areas and food stocks. The Borders, never a wealthy area, also suffered from general poverty and bad roads, which combined to worsen the situation. A bad harvest in the Borders might be localised, but with poor roads impassable due to autumn storms, little relief could be brought in from other areas. Even when journeys could be attempted, with no produce to sell, the Borderers had no money to buy. This was further exacerbated by the desperate and the ruthless, who raised prices. Farm labourers with no savings and existing debt were at most risk, while those with some savings could quickly see their funds spent. In certain dire circumstances, assets were sold, reducing tenant farmers to labourers as the rent for farm tenancies could not be paid.

Whatever the cause, in addition to disease, famine was also seen as a punishment from God or an attack by the Devil. Where harvest failure was localised, such as occurred in the Borders, a community could add the fear of attack by Auld Nick to the misery of starvation. While the Kirk interpreted this as 'proof' of their Godliness, it is unlikely that after repeated bouts of famine the local populace found any solace in that spiritual notion.

While Borderers were trying to survive, they also had to contend with riders from Edinburgh seeking to buy or steal what they needed for the hungry mouths in the capital. When a bad harvest struck and food stocks in Edinburgh ran low, the city fathers would authorise the forced buying of grain and livestock from the rural hinterlands of Mid, West and East Lothian and the Borders. However, not all of those that arrived from Edinburgh offered a fair price, with many offering under market value, rarely enough for farmers to cover their costs and their own stocks were low. But refusal to sell frequently resulted in grain and livestock being taken without any payment. The authorities in Edinburgh, always afraid of the mob, needed to feed the city no matter what. The troops sent out were under orders that if food could not be bought, it was to be taken. The Borders Kirk railed against this injustice, seeing in it the hand of the Devil as people in the Borders starved to death.

The work of Auld Nick was not done and the following years of the century saw plague and famine return several more times.

Rural life was disrupted as those who were ill or caring for the sick or dying could not plough fields or attend to livestock. Untended livestock strayed from their home fields never to be found, eating crops that could not be harvested. The normal rhythms of rural life – including attending the Kirk – became disordered, further unsettling the local clergy. Some individuals even left the area. On the surface of it, this seems a reasonable response to what must have seemed an almost unremitting catalogue of disasters. But to leave a tight-knit rural Borders community in the 17th century was, however, almost unheard of, and to do so was to instantly arouse suspicion. If, after an individual left a village, conditions improved, then the suspicion was that the emigrant had been the cause of the ill fortune. On the other hand, if conditions worsened, it was often thought that the individual had caused the misfortune and then left to avoid its consequences. Either way the family left behind could bear the brunt of any lingering resentment.

Whether individuals left home with the blessing of their families or not, the Kirk saw in this act unnatural tendencies. Obedience to the family, to honour one's father and mother, was what was expected; not to abandon them in their time of need. Sons who dishonoured their parents were yet more proof that the Devil was walking abroad, sowing discord even within the family home. While leaving home was practically unheard of, arriving in a new location was fraught with danger as many in new communities were suspicious of strangers. Many of those who left found that the villages where they tried to settle would attempt to send them home again if they knew where they came from. In order to avoid this, wanderers often had to travel some distance to ensure anonymity. In the case of the Borders, this was more easily done due to their proximity to England. The Borders lost more young men in this way than any other region of Scotland.

In 1635, complete disaster struck and plague and famine came together. For many this was too much and, in many villages and towns, entire families succumbed to the double blow. Some smaller hamlets disappeared altogether, the effects of plague and the failure of the harvest proving overwhelming for small communities. The strong frequently survived periods of little food; however, malnutrition makes the body susceptible to illness and disease, a vulnerability that could last for two or three years after the actual famine had passed. This could result in the death of stronger, fitter individuals, especially in prolonged periods of poor harvests or when famine years came close together. This, then, reduced the number of fit individuals able to work on the land, placing further strain on an already weakened community. In addition, villages tended at that time to consist of a limited number of families. Within those households were certain key individuals; a miller for grinding wheat and baking bread in the communal oven, or a smith for repairing farming implements. If an individual with these vital skills died, a village might struggle to survive. In previous years, a nearby village's miller might be employed but when, in addition to these deaths movement was also restricted, this might prove a tipping point where life in the village became unsustainable.

The loss of communities that had existed for generations was unsettling to the surrounding villages and increased fears within the clergy. Repeated years of famine and plague were even starting to erode faith in the ability of the clergy to protect the populace from attacks by the Devil. The Kirk's response was to increase the search for and prosecution of witches. In 1640, the General Assembly of the Kirk of Scotland passed the first of its Condemnatory Acts against witches. This was followed by another Condemnatory Act in 1643 and a third in 1644.[8]

Unfortunately for the Kirk, Auld Nick did not seem to be too troubled by these Acts – at least not in the Borders. In 1644, barely a matter of weeks after the passing of the third Condemnatory Act, plague and famine once again hit the Borders together. Although several areas of Scotland also suffered one of these blights that year, it was only in the Borders that the two had come together. Murmurs rose again about the Kirk's inability to protect its flock which, although understandable given the circumstances, merely added to the clergy's belief in the diabolical nature of the events. To question the authority of the Kirk was in itself seen as an act of blasphemy. Pressure from the Borders Kirk led to the passing of yet another Condemnatory Act against witches in 1645. This Act appeared to work and for the next four years the Borders remained disease free and with a healthy crop at harvest.

But although free from famine, hunger remained a problem that year. The armies of the Royalists and the Covenanters were in the Borders; armies that needed feeding. The official policy might have been to pay local farmers for their produce, but on the ground soldiers more often than not – and frequently under the orders of local commanders – just took what was necessary. Retreating troops, on whatever side, would also employ the scorched earth policy of torching fields as they went to leave no supplies for pursuing armies. The battle of Philiphaugh near Selkirk in September 1645 may have been famous for the destruction of the Covenanter army of Sir David Leslie and infamous for the slaughter of the camp followers, but locally it was notorious for the destruction of the year's harvest and theft of livestock that left many in Selkirk short that winter.

At last, a year without plague, famine or soldiers came in 1646. But those soldiers who had caused such shortages now needed to be paid and the money to pay them came from taxes levied on all. 'Good' years, such as 1646, saw farmers faced with taxes that left them with less money to buy new stock. Mortality rates remained high. The beleaguered Kirk responded by passing yet another Condemnatory Act in the spring of 1649.

Finally, things appeared to improve but it is estimated that as much as 15 per cent of the Borders population died, and that Europe as a whole lost two million people to famine in the 17th century.

These repeated cycles of plague and famine, which were common in rural communities across Europe throughout the century, were sufficiently severe as to make many question their cause. Combined with civil war, revolution and the execution of a King, these disasters readily fed into and supported the belief that the Borders was under attack from Auld Nick.

But, as in all human societies, the events in 17th century Scotland did not occur in a vacuum. Existing beliefs and previous experiences coloured how events in the Borders were interpreted, and if the 17th century was the time of witch burnings, then the 16th century had been the time of the reivers. The memory of the reivers and their bloody ways remained strong in the Borders.

An area that had seen reivers, wars, plague and famine was clearly the target of the Devil and his ilk. The new century would see the union of the Parliaments and the flowering of the Scottish Enlightenment. In the Borders, the beginning of the 18th century saw the burning of Meg Lawson at the top of the Gallows Knowe in Selkirk for the 'wicked cryme of witchcraft'.

3

Peebles, 1629

'vehementlie suspect of wytchcraft'

PEEBLES IN THE 17th century was a relatively prosperous small town, sitting as it did beside the river Tweed and on one of the main trading roads to Edinburgh. Well-off and well educated, this was not a town that succumbed to the ignorant superstitions of its rural cousins; or so the people of Peebles confidently thought. The town had been made a Royal Burgh in 1152 by King David 1, and saw itself as a place of substance. The minister of the town would talk of the witches caught further east and south in the Borders and warn his flock to be ever vigilant. This was thought typical of the wild debatable lands of reiver country, not the lush green calm of Peebles. And then 1629 dawned and that calm was broken.

The spring had been particularly soft that year and the nights pleasant and mild. It was thought that the summer would be a good one and produce a good harvest. The farm labourers and middling folks (the better off merchants and farmers that would roughly approximate a middle class) of Peebles predicted a prosperous year. After a long day's work, men and women gathered in doorways and lanes to talk and pass the day's news. May blossom floated on the breeze as neighbour nodded to neighbour, noting who was here and there and what was what. As the days passed, however, the evening chat turned to gossip as suspicious late-night gatherings were seen and noted. Why did Katherine Wode and Marion Boyd always hurry so down towards the Tor Hill ignoring their neighbours' greetings? And why did Patrick Lintoun yawn all the morning, barely able to keep his eyes open, when he should surely have been abed all night? Idle curiosity was slowly turning into speculation when Marion Boyd, Gilbert Hog and Janet Hendersoun missed the Kirk service two Sundays in a row. In the febrile atmosphere of the 17th century, this was highly suspicious. This sin of omission was further compounded when all three claimed to have been ill, but had been seen on both Sundays out on the drover's road – where they had no business to be – looking hale and hearty, albeit somewhat furtive.

It is not known exactly when the word 'witch' was first uttered, or who first whispered it, but once mentioned, under the breath and with a cautious look over the shoulder, there could be no stopping the consequences. It was well known that the previous winter, when many had been ill, Bessie Ur and Margaret Gowanlock had tended to the sick. And then it was also remembered that neither Bessie nor Margaret had fallen ill themselves, but several that they had tended had in fact died. The neighbours of William Thomesoun now recalled a quarrel that had resulted in a good horse going lame just when it was needed. More rumours were spoken abroad and further accusations started to fly; as did some of the accused. Marion Crosier, Gilbert Hog and Margaret Dicksoun fled the town, adding to the gossip. More names were whispered and eventually the presbytery of Peebles met to discuss the matter. Several townsfolk were called in to answer questions and the meeting lasted well into the night. When the presbytery rose in the early hours of the morning, the minister had a list of 27 names.

Agnes Chalmers; Sussanna Elphinstoun; Margaret Yerkine; William Thomesoun; William Mathesoun; Thomas Stoddart; Agnes Robesoun; Katherine Broun; Marie Johnestoun; Janet Hendersoun; Agnes Thomesoun; Katherine Wode; Marion Crosier; Issobel Haddock; Gilbert Hog; Jean Watsoun; Margaret Dicksoun; Margaret Johnestoun; Janet Achesoun; Bessie Ur; Katherine Alexander; Helen Beatie; Margaret Gowanlock; Marion Boyd; Katherine Mairschell; Patrick Lintoun; and John Graham, known as 'Joke the Graham'. Every one of them was a resident of Peebles; although some had family connections as far away as Dalkeith and Glasgow. Known to the Minister and the Kirk elders, all those named were noted to be 'vehementlie suspect of wytchcraft'. The presbytery wrote immediately to the Privy Council in Edinburgh for a Commission to try sundry witches in the parish. Within the week, the Commission giving the baillies and sheriffs of Peebles, Dalkeith and Glasgow permission to 'search for, apprehend, arrest and interrogate said accused persones' had been received. The interrogation of the accused was to take place within 15 days of the arrest.[9]

The town was in an uproar. Twenty-seven had been named; not even the worst town gossips had guessed at that number. Doors were shut fast and evening chats became a thing of the past. Attendance at the Kirk on Sunday was strictly adhered to by all, even the frail and the sick. In the town, the sheriff deputised more men and the search began. Almost all of the accused had fled once their names were made known. Some of them had made it as far as Innerleithen. One was apprehended on the road to Biggar, but soon all were rounded up and brought back to Peebles. There was not enough room for all of them in the town's tolbooth and several were locked in the Kirk as the investigation began. The charges were similar in all cases: that they had met at night for nefarious purposes; that they had made a compact with the Devil and denied their baptism; that they had frolicked with Auld Nick; and that he had helped them to lay sickness on various neighbours, some of whom had died as a result. These pacts were the worst of charges; this was not a case of one old woman using charms to cure illness, but a mass worshipping of the Devil. The charges were put to all 27 and all denied them.

The minister, Archibald Syd, had been horrified at the apparent extent of witchcraft in his town and was determined to get to the truth of the matter. Questioning of the suspects began immediately and continued day after day and night after night. The baillie's men working in shifts round the clock ensured that the accused were allowed no sleep. The Kirk elders terrified by this outbreak of apparent Devil worship quoted texts and condemned the accused for their actions. Determined to root out this evil, they questioned the accused repeatedly going over every detail of the accusations. Issobel Haddock, described in the court records as 'a young girl', was the first to confess. Finally succumbing to pressure, she admitted all: yes, she had gone to a meeting on the Tor Hill; yes, the Devil had been there; yes, there were others there; yes, she knew them; and yes, the ultimate proof, she would name them.

And with this first confession, all the others broke down and also confessed. Tumbling over each other, they told of what they had done, what they had said and who they had seen.

Further details poured out: what the Devil looked like, what his voice was like and what he had promised them. Shrieking agreement to whatever question was put to them, many of the accused became hysterical and their shouts and screams could be heard outside in the streets. Baillie's men had to be posted outside the tolbooth to keep the curious away. Armed with the initial confessions, Syd and the elders started to question the accused more closely about what had happened with the Devil before turning to witnesses in the town about what they knew of the matter. When the elders started their questioning of the town an immediate division arose. Half the town had tales to tell. Accusation were made, some direct and some vague. Stories were remembered and anecdotes created. Everyone had 'known for years' that this one or that one was suspect. The rest of the town denied everything. Made up predominantly of friends and relatives of the accused, they stood firm in the face of prolonged questioning. They were lucky, none were arrested, as often happened to the families of accused witches. After two days of questioning, the elders had heard more than enough. They had sufficient evidence with which to proceed to trial and the court date was duly set for 11 June.

The main room of the tolbooth was crowded even before the accused were brought in. The jury of townsmen of good character, who had been selected by the presbytery, sat together on a double row of wooden benches. The Kirk elders sat before a table containing several manuscripts and a Bible. Another table was occupied by the prosecutors and a third by the court clerk. The back of the room was filled with various townsfolk, some curious, most fearful. At the front of the room were a number of low stools for the accused. When the suspected witches were brought in it was discovered that there were not enough stools for all of them to sit down and some were forced to sit on the stone floor. Some were weeping, some sat dejected and others seemed oblivious to the whole affair playing with the ends of their hair or staring vacantly around them at the curious spectators. Once everyone was assembled, the minister rose and facing the crowd read out the long list of charges and confessions laid against each of the accused.

The speed with which the accused had gone from being free men and women to being arrested, charged and interrogated seemed

to have rendered them unable to contemplate even a token protest. Although a formal defence was allowed, no advocate spoke
on their behalf. They were quite alone. After the charges were read,
the minister turned to speak in detail about each of the accused.
Various witnesses were called to confirm what they could about
the charges laid against the suspect. Questions were put about the
accused's reputation. Previous bad character was discussed and any
lack of attendance at the Kirk was confirmed by the elders. This
was repeated for each of the accused and then the minister charged
the jury with their duty. The jury deliberated for a few minutes
and then wrote their decision down before handing the paper to
the minister. The trial was over and had taken less than a day. The
verdicts and sentences seemed an almost foregone conclusion. The
minister rose and started to read out the verdict for each. Agnes
Chalmers, guilty; Patrick Lintoun, guilty; Margaret Yerkine, guilty;
and so on until 24 names had been called. Sussanna Elphinstoun,
Margaret Johnestoun and Joke the Graham were not named in the
decision.[10] The minister challenged the jury who stated that they
found the charges against the three not to be proven. Elphinstoun,
Johnestoun and Graham were returned to the keeping of the baillie until a further decision could be made regarding their fate. The
lead Commissioner pronounced the death sentence on all of their
colleagues, including young Issobel Haddock. Five days later, the
24 witches were walked, barefoot and bareheaded, up to the Calf
Knowe, worriet and then burned in tar barrels. Arrest to execution
had taken less than 21 days.

The next session of the presbytery, however, was not a contented one. If 24 were guilty, how could the case against the other
three be not proven? Under Scots law up to the beginning of the
17th century there was a distinct two verdict system. Juries in
criminal trials decided if an accused were 'guilty' or 'not guilty'.
By the 17th century, however, judges were keen to temper the
power of juries, especially as they had an annoying habit of finding Covenanters, that the Crown wanted to punish, not guilty.
As a result, Scottish judges began restricting the jury's role to
deciding whether specific factual allegations were 'proven' or 'not
proven' and then the judge could decide whether to convict. The
Commissioner in this case could have simply convicted on the not

proven verdicts but it seems that Archibald Syd was not content with that. Perhaps the sheer number of accused or the seriousness of the Devil allegations drove him to want a more solid statement of guilt from the jury. Whatever the reason, the presbytery of Peebles applied to the Privy Council for a further Commission to re-try the remaining three accused witches. Until the Commission was received, Sussanna, Margaret and Joke the Graham were kept in custody. Unluckily for them, the Privy Council was, at that time, busy with Commissions for several other Borders towns and they sat out the summer and autumn incarcerated in the town's tolbooth awaiting a second trial.

By the time the Commission was finally received it was December and the trial was held on the 22nd day of the month. The same charges were brought, the same evidence produced and then the confessions and guilty verdicts of the former 24 was used as further evidence against Sussanna, Margaret and Joke the Graham. Their friendship with known witches who had, in some cases, named them as being present at their meetings with the Devil was emphasised. These were added to the existing charges against the three accused, as was the fervent condemnation of Archibald Syd. The former jury were brought back, under pressure no doubt to correct their previous mistaken verdict. Susanna, Margaret and Joke the Graham had, by then, spent over six months in gaol on poor food, no exercise and with no sanitation. The psychological stress of their situation and its almost inevitable outcome had also left its mark and their appearance at the trial showed three individuals who looked, smelled and possibly acted exactly as Auld Nick's followers would. As before, the trial took barely a day, and on this occasion all three were found guilty and instantly sentenced to death. The order was sent again to the baillie and his men to 'prepare them for death'.[11] They were worriet and burned on Christmas Eve with the minister leading his flock directly from the execution site to the Kirk for the midnight service to celebrate Christ's birth.

During the 17th century, the Presbyterian Kirk in Scotland was struggling to assert itself and define its final form. The young faith was in danger from all sides as the Devil used all his wiles to attack them; most notably giving succour to those stubbornly remaining Catholic in their beliefs and employing women as witches. It was this double threat that occupied the minds of the Kirk in the Borders as they fought for their very survival. The Reformation that had been sparked by Martin Luther's protests at the worst excesses of certain members of the Catholic Church had swept across Europe with a speed that had surprised all including Luther. The idea that the church needed to reform itself and regain its initial Christian ideals had caught the imagination of all and had excited many. New ideals and theologies were discussed and debated and new reform leaders sprang up; Jean Calvin, Martin Bucer, Huldrych Zwingli. But as these leaders protested about the church's many abuses, the Counter-Reformation arose to defend the Catholic faith against what was seen as a dangerous attack on Christianity itself. Jesuits Francisco Ribera and Robert Bellarmine rose to defend mother church. Before long, zealots on both sides were accusing the other of being in the pay of the Devil and the opposing faith became not a different form of Christianity but Devil worship. For Catholics, the Protestants were attacking mother church, which had been founded by St Peter, and the pope, whose primacy and apostolic succession came from Saint Peter. What else could Protestants be but the foot soldiers of the Devil? The Protestant camp viewed the Catholics as those who had betrayed Christ by allowing his church to be corrupted by wealth and power. The selling of indulgences to wash away one's sins had put the very grace of the Lord up for sale. This could only have been the work of the Devil.

The Reformation and Counter-Reformation saw physical and theological battles fought across Europe including Scotland. By the arrival of the 17th century, Scotland had settled into the new faith; the true faith. And yet there were those that stubbornly refuse to accept this. In the eyes of many in the Kirk, Catholic resistance was more than just a refusal to accept a new form of worship, it was an affront to God and as such must be inspired by the Devil. Rituals and incantations muttered in Latin and the mysteries of the mass came to be thought of as having more than a whiff of brimstone about them. The fresh ideals of the Reformation quickly became bogged down in mistrust and hatred as the remaining Catholics clung tenaciously to their faith.

The Borders held few Catholics but their very scarcity merely heightened the conviction that their beliefs were superstitious in the extreme. But there was one place where there were a lot of Catholics and unfortunately it was just across the national border. When England had broken with Rome in the rule of Henry VIII, the north of England, and particularly the north east, had remained Catholic. For a variety of reasons, both the nobility and the peasantry of Northumbria had remained loyal to Rome. The Catholics of the north of England were, in the minds of the Borders ministers and elders, a terrifying reminder of the power of Auld Nick. As in all border regions, tales were told of atrocities and terrors just over 'there'. Outsiders were suspect and, in this case, they were English and Catholic so viewed as doubly untrustworthy. Few Borderers travelled far from home at that time and the few traders who did venture down to markets in Berwick-upon-Tweed or Alnwick would return with tales to tell. Some true and some, no doubt, exaggerated as traveller's tales often are, they nevertheless fed into the common perceptions of the 'foreignness' of Catholics. Stories of drunken behaviour or purses that were stolen that could equally be told about Edinburgh or Glasgow would, in this case, 'prove' the diabolical nature of Catholics. For the ministers and elders of the Borders Kirk, the presence of these English Catholics was a nest of vipers that lay too close for comfort.

The Protestant establishment, determined to destroy the Catholic faith in Scotland or at the very least break its power, described Catholic beliefs as superstition. The Witchcraft Act of 1563 outlawed superstition and superstitious practices by the people, but it was left to the Kirk to define those superstitions. Known Catholics with their beliefs were easily identified but scarce in the Borders. However, what about those who merely followed the beliefs handed down to them by grandparents? Half-remembered responses from the Catholic mass or prayers to the Virgin Mary for help were now devilish superstition rather than harmless folk beliefs. And it was women that used these charms and lucky amulets; and women were the second part of the threat perceived by the Borders Kirk.

The domestic world, the domain of women, was an area where women held authority. That sat uneasily with the Kirk and its teachings. Dominated by men whose views on women were typical of Europe at the time, these teachings would have horrific consequences. While men were sometimes arrested and tried as witches, the majority of those accused were women. In Scotland as a whole, around 84 per cent of those suspected were women; in the Borders, the figure was even higher at 92 per cent of known cases. But why should this be? Why were women believed to be witches in such large numbers? The reason goes back to early beliefs anent women and their inferiority to and difference from men.

The *Malleus Maleficarum*,[12] the great guide to witches and their ways, written by Kramer, a Dominican monk in the late 16th century, outlined in detail why women were more susceptible to witchcraft. The *Malleus* started with the statement that there was no point offering the opinion that there were not more female witches than male as it was patently true by anyone and everyone's observation. After this opening certainty, the book outlined, at great length, the reasons why. It was a commonly held belief that women did not know how to be moderate in their goodness or their wickedness and when they passed the boundaries of their proper status, they became extremely wicked. Kramer quoted various sources for this belief, from Roman historians such as Seneca to Christian scholars such as St Augustine and then finally the scriptures themselves.

Kramer's work also built on the commonly held belief that women were inclined to be gullible and naive and were thus easier to trick than men. The Devil, whose main aim was to destroy the true faith, would then use women as they were more trusting; they could not see past his tricks. And again, Kramer quoted scripture to prove his point. Women were also physically weak. Their bodies leaked; menstrual blood and breast milk were the sure signs of a leaky and thus weak vessel. As their bodies were weak so, it followed, was their faith. When attacked by the Devil, they were too weak to resist and so became one of his followers. Even when they could resist, their weak nature made them more impressionable. Easily swayed by the lies of the Devil, they were used in his evil plans. Another problem with women was that they had a 'lewd and slippery' tongue. This made them natural bedfellows for the Prince of Lies and well able to spread lies for their diabolical master.

As if this were not enough, women were also thought to be extremely lustful and given to carnal filthiness. This was supposed to have derived from women being created from Adam's rib.

It was thought that as the part of the rib used had curved away from Adam's body and away from his true godly heart it had left women unfinished and thus weak, depraved and given to deceit. Kramer used the derivation of the word *femina* to support this idea. Kramer explained that *fe* meant faith and *minus* meant less, meaning that women had less faith than men. What faith they did have, according to Kramer's logic, they were less able to keep. According to the beliefs of the day, a wicked woman, because of her poor character, would waver in her belief and would both quickly and easily deny her faith and this denial was the very foundation of her witchcraft.

Women were also castigated for their basic character. It was believed that women, when they hated someone they had previously loved, seethed and raged with hatred. This emotional excess made them seek revenge on anyone who had wronged them. This excess also saw women take disproportionate revenge on those whom they believed had wronged them. A minor domestic dispute would be escalated into employing the Devil to wreak one's revenge. Women were also thought to have a defective memory, be impulsive and had a lack of sense of duty. They forgot their Christian teaching, they rose quickly to anger and easily dismissed their duty to God; all of which led them to a life of service with the Devil. Even a woman's voice was likened to the deadly song of the sirens, able to kill men and make them deny God.

The *Malleus* stated the fears about women and authority that Knox would pursue some 70 years later and would be continued by the Kirk. If women were in control of men then disaster would strike. Their bodies and personalities were weak, deformed even, and susceptible to the blandishments of the Devil. Their gait, posture and dress were designed to seduce men. They were carnal and lustful and were never sexually satisfied: this inability to be satisfied led them to arouse themselves with evil spirits. Copulation with Auld Nick was recorded in many of the Scottish witchcraft trials.

And what of women who were witches – what was believed of them? It was generally believed that three main vices held sway in women and even more so in wicked women. They had a lack of faith, were licentious and had self-interest. The logic of the day stated that women applied themselves to witchcraft more than men because, unlike men, they were prey to those particular vices. Licentiousness was considered to be the most dominant of the vices. Selfish women were most deeply infected with evil if they also had uncontrollable lust. Seven kinds of evil magic were listed by the church which involved sex in one form or other. The first was by magically making people want excessive sex. It was generally believed that men were weak where sex was concerned and that women could, and did, entice them into having excessive sex. The church authorities were concerned that men would become blinded by lust and neglect their duties both spiritual and temporal. Sex was, of course, necessary for procreation and as such was tolerated by the Kirk. Sex for enjoyment, even within marriage, was considered extremely sinful and was blamed on women who had lured their husbands into sin.

In contrast, the next form of magic was causing impotency. This was a huge concern to the church and to society as a whole. Impotent men could not father children – more importantly, sons – and this was considered to be a non-natural state that had to be the result of witchcraft. Marriage, after all, had been instigated by God as a means of continuing the human race. Human biology was poorly understood at that time, with reproduction no exception. Male impotency, which can have many causes, was considered so serious that it was one of the few grounds on which a wife could divorce a husband. The damage to the male ego caused by an inability to father sons was only slightly mitigated by an accusation of witchcraft but that did at least lay the blame where it belonged, with the witch not the man.

The third kind of evil magic was even worse: shrinking or removing a man's penis. This was a belief strongly held by the people. Witches were thought to beguile men by offering extreme pleasure the price for which was the actual loss of manhood. No recorded cases of this appear in the witchcraft trials in the Borders; however, fears around the male sexuality ran deep. The fear of castration, in any form, was not only an issue for the male psyche but as man had been made in God's image, any deviation from that image could be construed as blasphemous; especially if it was the result of the actions of a woman.

The next was changing people into animals for sexual purposes. The *Malleus* talked at length on the issue of incubi and succubi, the demons that tormented people at night to have intercourse with them. But rural people working with animals all day were more likely to dream of horses or dogs than mythical demonic creatures. But horse or incubus, someone had to be blamed for the unwanted pregnancy of an unwed woman. For a man, being found *in flagrante delicto* with a sheep was less shaming if you claimed you had been bewitched and turned into a ram.

The fifth type of magic was making women barren and the next was causing miscarriages. These were the two charges that were frequently laid at the door of midwives. As childbearing was the natural order of things, a married woman who did not have children or who miscarried was believed to have been bewitched. In previous times, prayers to the Virgin for babies was perfectly normal. For those who had suffered miscarriages and stillbirths, penances and sometimes a pilgrimage might be undertaken. But the Reformation had removed that positive emotional release from the sorrow of childlessness and replaced it with the negative emotional belief that the lack of children was being caused by a bewitchment.

The final magical act was sacrificing small children to the Devil. This macabre crime could either be carried out by killing a child and using its body or by digging up an existing dead child. In either case, body parts, most notably bones, were offered to the Devil and sometimes ground up for use in ointments or in rituals. There are no instances of this actual accusation being levelled at anyone in the Scottish Borders but it was a commonly held belief about what witches did. Indeed, there were few instances of any of these beliefs playing a role in the accusation within the Scottish trials. What they were, however, was a set of generally held beliefs about witches which added to the fears of the times. Sex was at the heart of all of these magical practices, not because the Kirk or society was obsessed with sex per se but because sex was important. Without sex, there were no children; without children, society, including the Kirk, would end. For rural communities who frequently lived life on the precarious edge of starvation, childlessness was much more than a personal tragedy for those personally involved. A lack of children in a village meant a lack of hands to work the land and could mean the difference between the survival of an entire community and its destruction. For the Kirk, too, a lack of children was of vital importance. The new faith, God's Kirk could not remain strong without soldiers to defend it from the Devil's attacks.

That the faith was under attack was not in doubt. That women were potentially wicked was not in doubt. Putting the two together, the Borders Kirk had cause and effect identified and thus looked no further. Borders witches also faced the belief among many in the Kirk that the more godly the Kirk, the greater the ferocity of the Devil's attack. This self-fulfilling prophesy in the Borders presbyteries saw the more godly the minister, the more witches there would be in any local community. With the Kirk in control of the investigations into suspected witches, the number could only increase. Equally, as ministers led the interrogation of suspected witches then the fate of those witches became in most cases a foregone conclusion. The presence of a witch proved how godly the local minister was and, therefore, how truthful he was; the truthfulness of the minister 'proved' the witch to be guilty. The greater the number of witches in a community, the greater its Godliness. For why else would the Devil attack them? While the Kirk fought Auld Nick and all his followers it was local communities that suffered. Taught by the social fabric of village life what the moral code was, lectured from the pulpit on the dangers of women and surrounded and attacked by plague and famine and war, local communities had only one saviour and that was the Kirk.

As the women were accused, the men rose to the challenge and defended their Kirk. In the Border records that exist, the same names reappear time and time again: Hume, Pringle, Scott, Veitch and Cleland. Men that were uncompromising in their faith, men that would, in their time, face gaol rather than accept anything less than a pure Presbyterian faith. These were men who investigated and interrogated witches not only in their own parishes but in neighbouring communities and further afield. They would travel the length and breadth of the Borders to help their brother ministers in their times of trouble, helping to consign to the flames the witches that threatened their Kirk. And it was not just ministers but local Commissioners who also rose to the challenge. Landowners whose younger brothers had entered the ministry sat in judgement of the Borders women and again the same names appear: Pringle, Scott and Hume. Ministers and Commissioners came from the same families ensuring 'guid men' ran the trials. For the accused, however, this removed any chance to challenge as no Commissioner would doubt the word of a minister who was his brother or cousin. The Borders sat secure in the knowledge that accusations would be swiftly followed by sentences of execution. When the circuit courts travelled the Borders to undertake trials, the magistrates travelled too; stout defenders of the Kirk.

The Borders Kirk, proud inheritors of the independent Borders spirit, had seen their communities attacked by the Devil and knew their time had come. They were God's Elect and this was their mission to drive witches from the face of the earth. Their zeal would consign 221 to the flames, some would die in gaol from their torture and treatment and still others would commit suicide.

4

Melrose, 1629

'four guid men'

ON 1 AUGUST 1629, the Privy Council in Edinburgh received a request for a Commission to try four witches: Thomas Richartson and Helene Scot of Maxtoun; Margaret Patersoun of Langnewtoun and Helen Gastoun of Lassuden. The request was signed by John Halliburton of Murruslaw, Baillie of Melrose; Sir Thomas Ker of Cavers, Sheriff of Teviotdale; Andrew Ker of Maisondieu, Baillie of Selkirk; and James Pringle of Buckholme, Baillie of Melrose.[13]

The four had come under suspicion for the usual list offences: an evil look here and there, Margaret Patersoun had caused chickens to stop laying and Thomas Richartson was absent from the Kirk without good reason. But what had caused the greatest outrage was their attitude to the local authorities. When Helen Gastoun and Helene Scot, the two alleged leaders of the group, were warned that their names were being bandied about as witches, Helene Scot had stated that she cared nothing for the accusations, the accusers and the authorities who believed such 'fool's blether'. Helen Gastoun had gone further declaring that the Baillie was himself a fool and no more able to catch a witch than wring a chicken's neck. This disrespect soon reached the ears of John Halliburton and James Pringle and confirmed all the accusations they had heard. The request to the Privy Council was hastily written and sent up to Edinburgh. Richartson, Patersoun, Scot and Gastoun were all arrested and locked up in the Baillie's house in Melrose.

All four were noted to be poor labouring folk of the local area. The friendship between the four appeared to rest on their alleged witchcraft as no family relationship could be found. They all lived about three miles of each other in the rich farmland a few miles to the south-east of Melrose. The records of the 1629 case shed little light on the actual trial and the fate of the accused. Their alleged crimes have not warranted extensive records although the accusations laid were serious enough for the Privy Council to grant a Commission in the first place. The full trial records have been lost over the years but what has not been lost are some curious facts regarding the four Commissioners.

James Pringle of Buckholme in Gallowshiels was Commissioner in 17 trials between 1629 and 1630. Although being a baillie of Melrose, Pringle was involved in trials in Selkirk and Berwick. In over 80 per cent of Pringle's cases the accused were executed. Thomas Ker of Cavers, Sheriff of Teviotdale was involved in 20 cases between 1629 and 1649. He was involved in cases across Selkirk, Melrose, Jedburgh, Berwickshire and East Lothian. He was frequently involved in cases where the accused had refused to confess and where the evidence presented was slight. In 90 per cent of the cases in which he was involved, the accused were executed. On several occasions Pringle and Thomas Ker recommended each other for duty as Commissioners. Andrew Ker of Maisondieu was the son of Thomas Ker and sat as a Commissioner in 12 cases in 1629. John Haliburton was involved in four trials in 1629.

It should be noted that all witchcraft trial Commissioners were paid for their time from an initial accusation until the final execution. They were the only individuals, apart from witch brodders, who made money out of the trials. Their claim for payment for the work undertaken in this matter was always paid first out of the local funds. Where funds were not available, some communities took out loans to pay the Commissioners and in some instances Commissioners took the local community to court to force payment.

The Commissioners that presided over witch interrogation and trials in the Borders were all local landowners. They were known to the local minister as 'guid men' and thus capable of sitting in judgement on others. What they were not was lawyers. Few, if any, of them had received any training in the law; that was not considered necessary. They were chosen by the local minister because they were men of good character and thus capable, in his opinion, of rendering a fair judgement. This system had grown out of various elements of local justice that had developed across Scotland over the centuries. A practical response to the geography of the land and grown out of the clan and family system it had initially served reasonably well but had one fatal weakness. It was self-regulating. And like all closed, self-regulating systems, it was easily corrupted. By the 17th century and the loss of the Parliament to London, the system was entirely under the control of the Kirk.

An accusation was made to the minister. The minister would then ask a local landowner, a 'guid man', to write to the Privy Council for a Commission to try the witch. This Commission, usually headed by the local minister, would test the accusation before deciding to take the accused to court. The Privy Council issued the Commission but did not appoint the Commissioner – that was a local matter. Edinburgh did not interfere. On receiving the Commission, the minster would approach other 'guid men' to act as Commissioners. Who else but the ultimate 'guid man' of the parish would be qualified to recommend an individual as a Commissioner? On the next occasion a witch was to be tried, the same 'guid men' would be approached. If an individual was unable to act due to other commitments, one 'guid man' could recommend another but the final selection was made by the minister. Commissioners that gave out lenient sentences were few and far between and those that did would be quickly dropped from the minister's list of those on whom he could call. Those Commissioners who wanted to retain the minister's good will and their local reputation, which of course depending in no small part to the minister's attitude, would realise that a severe sentence was always the preferred option. This, obviously, resulted in the most severe sentences becoming the normal practice.

In some instances, cases could be dismissed if no 'guid men' were available. In 1606, Issobell Falconner of Aymouth (Eyemouth) was accused of witchcraft. Before the case came to court, Issobell petitioned the Privy Council to dismiss the charges against her on the grounds that the sheriff-depute of Berwick and the Commissioners were not fit persons to try so high a crime. The sheriff-depute and Commissioners challenged this on the grounds that they were 'gentilmen of gude qualities and conditions'.[14] The Privy Council agreed with Issobell and her case was held over until some 'fit persone'[15] could be found to try her. The case was finally held in 1624 when she was released with a caution as to her future behaviour.

But ministers could push matters even further than severe sentences. In some cases, the legal niceties were not adhered to and the accused could find themselves being tortured without the requisite permission having been obtained or interrogation begun before a Commission was received. In both cases, the Commissioners had the authority and duty to stop the proceedings. In no instances in any Borders witch Commission did this occur. The 'guid men' of the Borders followed the lead of their minister rather than their duty to dispense justice. Where minister and justice ran hand in hand, as had happened in previous centuries, the Commissioners sat in courts that punished the guilty and protected the innocent. In the 17th century, even in the most scrupulously fair witchcraft trials, the minster and justice could easily part company. Religious fervour and a desire to defeat the Devil would drive ministers to excess where the ends justified the means. Unfortunately, because the ministers appointed the 'guid men' there was no check on what the 'means' might entail.

Into this closed system intruded the unknown element of human nature. Most minsters were driven by a genuine belief in the need to protect society from the evil of Auld Nick. Some ministers took that short but fatal step from religious fervour to spiritual frenzy and were inspired to attack the Devil no matter the cost. In a reverse of the famous Benjamin Franklin quote, some ministers thought it was better that 100 innocent persons should suffer than one guilty person escape. While some Commissioners may have disagreed, none raised their voices in protest.

Most Commissioners were driven by a need to work with the Kirk to protect the community. Some discovered that sitting on a witch trial could bring rich rewards. There was the basic payment for their time which all Commissioners received and was a welcome supplement to their normal income. Some of the more petty-minded Commissioners were known to pad out the time they had spent on an interrogation and trial for as long as possible or to claim for excess food and stabling. The big prize, however, was the political capital that could be gained from sitting on a Commission.

Getting to know members of the Privy Council in Edinburgh, getting your name known as one of the 'guid men' of the Borders, being seen as capable of dealing with difficult cases all helped in the slippery world of politics. There are Commissioners named in some Border witch trials that had no geographical or family connection with the cases but seemed keen to be associated with them. These same Commissioners also appear in some of the trials held in Edinburgh, usually in the Justiciary Court populated by members of the Privy Council.

James Pringle of Buckholme sat as a Commissioner in several cases across the Borders between 1629 and 1630. His interest in witchcraft trials seems to have lessened from 1631 onwards when he spent an increasing amount of time visiting Edinburgh. In 1632 the King granted James the lands and barony of Forgund, Perthshire and in 1633 he became laird of Buckholme. By the time he died in 1647, James Pringle was one of the wealthiest men in the Borders.

In 1643, the election of Thomas Ker of Cavers for the post of sheriff of Teviotdale was contested in the Convention of Estates. Ker's involvement in a range of cases across the Borders had been resented by some of the other Borders nobility and an action was laid against him challenging his fitness for the office of sheriff. However, despite the alleged irregularities in Ker's recent actions, he was supported by several members of the Convention and was confirmed in his position.

> haveing seene and considered the commission given in by the sherriffe of Teviotdaill the convention finds that the commission given to the saids Sir Thomas Ker... is the more legall; and therfor ordanis thame onlie to sitt in this convention as commissioners for the sherrifdome of Roxburgh.[16]

Andrew Ker, son of Thomas, sat as a Commissioner in 12 cases only and John Haliburton was involved in four. However, both men were favoured after their involvement in the 1629 cases. The first few years of Charles I's reign were somewhat rocky and, in the Borders, this was associated with a spike in witchcraft accusations and trials. Steadfast men were required to keep order. Andrew was noted to be 'his father's son' and in the years after 1629 extended his land at Maisondieu near Kelso. John was also recognised for his work and gained a considerable parcel of land adjoining James Pringle's land at Buckholme.

In contrast to the fortunes of the Commissioners, in 1650 one Agnes Gastoun of Melrose was apprehended and imprisoned 'for ane witche'.[17] Known as a quarrelsome dame she was apparently possessed of the evil eye. However, she was also recorded as being a destitute pauper. She was the daughter of the witch Helen Gastoun from Lassedun.

Given the Commissioners sitting on the case, the nature of the crimes and the attitudes of at least two of the accused it may be assumed that all four – Thomas Richartson, Helene Scot, Margaret Patersoun and Helen Gastoun – were found guilty of witchcraft and executed, although this cannot be known for certain.

5

Duns, 1630

'petition the King'

MARKET DAY IN Duns, December 1628, was abuzz with gossip about the goings on up in Haddington. Some vagabond had been arrested as a warlock and had named his witches. Ten had been named – 20, 30 – day after day, the story grew in the telling. Well what else could be expected of a beggar from East Lothian? They bred witches up there that tried to drown kings, everyone knew that.

The trials of the witches that had tried to sink the King's ship in 1590 had horrified everyone. The accused had given detailed confessions about their covens and witch's sabbats. They had talked of the spells that had cast and the demons they had summoned. They had confessed to promising to 'follow the De'il' and do his bidding. They had even met in the kirkyard of St Andrew's church to ply their filthy practices. The confessions were published in a pamphlet 'Newes from Scotland'[18] in 1591 which became regular reading in local marketplaces and inns across Scotland. For the majority of the populace, who were illiterate, the story was passed around fireplaces with some details embellished although little was needed. The involvement of Francis Stewart, 5th Earl of Bothwell, had added an extra frisson to the tale. Even the King had written about the witches in his great book on Daemonologie.[19] East Lothian became a byword for witchcraft.

As the new year dawned, more and more strange tales would filter down from the farmers and drovers that plied their trade between Duns and Haddington. One year on from the initial arrest, however, the good folk of Duns market would hear an accusation that would astound the whole of Berwickshire.

Duns was one of several small market towns in the county of Berwickshire in the early 1600s. Created a Burgh of Barony in 1489, the town held a weekly market on a Tuesday and once a month this was expanded as livestock were driven into the market square to be bought and sold. Sitting in the lush green of Berwickshire farm-land, Duns held the usual Borders mix of prosperous local nobility, tenant farmers and farm labourers, merchants dealing in wool and grain and the familiar rag tag of the poor and the destitute in the back alleys of the town. Market day would see them all rubbing shoulders, some to trade, a few to steal and most to gossip. The coming year would not disappoint.

Alexander Hammiltoun lived with a woman he called his wife in Haddington, East Lothian. Described variously as a vagabond and a beggar, he would regularly desert his wife to go wander-ing about the countryside in search of easy pickings and, some said, to escape her nagging tongue. Claiming to be originally from Durham or Newcastle or Gateshead, depending on his mood, Hammiltoun spent his time wandered the back roads of East Lothian and the Berwickshire coast. Occasionally traveling down as far as Tweedmouth and Berwick in England he would then turn back to places such as Prestonpans and Longniddry and some-times inland to Border towns like Duns.

As the winter of 1628 began to bite, Alexander started to head home to Haddington begging as he went. Somewhere in the flat-lands of East Lothian he had asked for alms and been refused. Hammiltoun, tired and hungry, had walked away with an ill grace muttering under his breath. Perhaps he spoke more loudly and aggressively then he intended, perhaps the householder had simply had their fill of beggars that day. Whatever the reason, the householder complained to the sheriff and Hammiltoun, already a marginal and thus suspicious character, was arrested. Most sher-iffs and baillies spent the late autumn months moving vagrants out of their jurisdictions before winter arrived. The Kirk might preach Christian charity but most merchants did not want more beggars on their streets and it was the merchants that paid the sheriff's wages. Beggars would be rounded up, spend a night in the tolbooth before being thrown out and told never to return the next morning. The last thing the Sheriff of Haddington wanted was a permanent resi-dent in his tolbooth but that is exactly what he got. Once word was out that the vagabond had been arrested, a torrent of accusations quickly followed, aided in no small part by Hammiltoun himself who seemed particularly keen to co-operate with the authorities. He named several local women as his accomplices and detailed their activities over the previous four years.[20]

Laying sickness, ruining crops, signing a pact with the Devil: there seemed no end to Hammiltoun's wickedness. A self-confessing witch, he should have been brought to trial relatively quickly but by December 1629, almost one whole year since his initial arrest, he was still sitting in Haddington tolbooth answering questions. What the local sheriff thought about this long-term resident is not known although, in similar cases, local merchants would frequently complain to the sheriff about the costs involved in guarding witches. Baillies and sheriffs ran up bills for food and bedding straw for the accused and arguments would rage about who was to pay. Bills would frequently not be paid for several months, if ever, after trials were over causing a great deal of ill feeling.

However, during his year-long stay, Hammiltoun continued to co-operate and the wealth of detail he produced was more than one investigator could handle. Several more were drafted in to help. One of them was Sir George Hume of Manderstoun, near Duns. Known for the thorough nature of his interrogations, Hume was detailed to investigate Hammiltoun's activities, most notably his pact with the Devil and the other witches with whom he associated. The investigation took several months, even with Hammiltoun's assistance, but slowly Sir George built up the detailed case in preparation for the inevitable trial. Sir George dismissed the most outlandish of Hammiltoun's claims. He knew from previous experience that some accused witches with nothing left to lose would revel in their notoriety making ever more extravagant confessions. Others would settle old scores by naming anyone they could think of partly out of spite but also to deflect attention from themselves. And there were also a few who went mad during their time in cold damp cells on a semi-starvation diet and with periodic torture. They would rant and rave about fantastical meetings with the Devil that had obviously never happened. Sir George was experienced enough to navigate between the different confessions he heard. He was not, however, prepared for the Hammiltoun's final confession. The vagabond from Haddington named Helen Arnot, Lady Manderstoun and Sir George's wife, as one of his fellow witches. According to Hammiltoun, Helen Arnot had come to him and asked him to help her ruin her husband's estate. Hammiltoun claimed to have resisted her and refused to help. He then stated that she had called on him again and this time asked for his help to murder her husband. This statement resulted in a torrent of questioning from Sir George but Hammiltoun refused to back down: Lady Manderstoun had asked for his help to bewitch her husband to death.[21]

Duns had never heard the like before. Neither had the local Kirk. Terrified by the prospect of offending a member of the nobility, but even more so of the unthinkable notion that she might be a witch, they quickly sought advice from the other local magistrates who all agreed: send the case to Edinburgh, let the Privy Council deal with the situation. No one in Berwickshire, it seems, wanted to deal with this case. Sir George was a powerful local landowner and Commissioner and now his own wife had been named for trying to kill him. While this dealt with the legalities of the case, it did little to calm the local community. Rumours, ever more unbelievable, soon started to circulate and a half-scared, half-curious crowd were soon circulating the Duns tolbooth in an attempt to see Hammiltoun. Servants at Manderstoun Hall, and anyone who had ever had any connection to Lady Arnot no matter how slight, regaled audiences in the local taverns receiving payment in tankards of ale. The message sent to the Privy Council detailed the delicacy of the case but also the need for prompt action to silence the local gossips.

On hearing the charges laid against her, Lady Manderstoun denied them all declaring them to be 'false and malicious'.[22] She is also said to have refused to appear before the court and to have threatened to have the court messenger, who had delivered the summons to her, whipped if she ever saw him again. Wiser counsel prevailed and nobody was whipped but, on her arrest, Lady Manderstoun demanded that Hammiltoun repeat his accusation before her. With powerful friends among the nobility she was not going to meekly submit to a trial. Demanding that Hammiltoun accuse her in person challenged the charge against her but also the court system; would they allow such an accusation to stand against a member of the nobility? The local magistrates hesitated. It was not normal for the accused to see their accuser until the trial. Using her influence, Lady Manderstoun then redoubled the pressure and managed to get the Privy Council to send for the witnesses to Hammiltoun's statement about Lady Manderstoun to give evidence.

On 3 December 1629, the Privy Council drew up an order for William Mowat and Patrick Abernathy the witnesses to Hammiltoun's statement to appear before the Council and give evidence.[23] William Mowat and Patrick Abernathy were investigators in the proceedings against Hammiltoun and had witnessed and recorded his accusations anent Helen. Both Mowat and Abernathy were servants of another of the trial investigators, James Mowat of Fawside. Mowat of Fawside was a writer to the Signet. The Society of Writers to His Majesty's Signet was formed in 1594 and comprised only 18 solicitors authorised to use the private seal of the King and to act as clerks to the courts. This was an extremely privileged position. Hammiltoun's accusation against Lady Manderstoun was now known at the highest level of Scottish society. However, both Mowat and Abernathy failed to appear before the Privy Council. Two weeks later, the Privy Council repeated their order for Mowat and Abernathy to come forward and give evidence. Yet again, neither man appeared and within the week they were both 'put to the horn'.[24]

Christmas was a bleak time for all that year: Lady Manderstoun remained under arrest suspected of witchcraft, all the while demanding to know by what right she was accused; Sir George had an ongoing witch investigation which now included a wife accused of trying to kill him; Mowat of Fawside faced explaining why his two servants had refused to give evidence; Mowat and Abernathy had disappeared and no one knew where they were and Alexander Hammiltoun still lay in Haddington tolbooth. The Privy Council were worried. Was Lady Manderstoun a witch? If she was not, then who was lying, Sir George or a writer to the Signet of both? Sir George and Mowat of Fawside had written statements as to Hammiltoun's accusation. There was no apparent solution that was not damaging. Unable to find an answer, the Privy Council tried to pass the buck. Writing to King Charles and presuming on his interest, if not knowledge (after all his father had written the Scottish book on witchcraft Daemonologie), they begged him to intervene. Charles was somewhat busy ruling England on his own after having dismissed his Parliament and failed to respond. The Privy Council would have to deal with the situation themselves.

By the first week in January, Mowat and Abernathy finally gave themselves up and confessed all to the Privy Council investigators who travelled down to Duns. Yes, they had heard Hammiltoun accuse Lady Manderstoun but they also told how he had been tortured and how both Mowat of Fawside and Sir George had questioned him privately just before his confession. The Privy Council had heard enough and stopped the questioning. William Mowat and Patrick Abernathy were both prosecuted for making false testimony against Lady Manderstoun.[25] Found guilty, they were sent out of Duns to Edinburgh to be imprisoned in the tolbooth.

Next to appear before the Privy Council was Hammiltoun. Brought from Haddington to Duns, he retracted his confession. He denied knowing Lady Manderstoun and that she had ever approached him to aid in the murder of her husband.[26] Dismissed, he was sent back to the tolbooth in Haddington to await the outcome of the remaining charges against him. The Privy Council, however, had greater problems with which to wrestle. They were convinced of Lady Manderstoun's innocence but they were equally puzzled by Hammiltoun's accusation. Such an obvious lie against a member of the nobility could only cause the vagabond trouble, so why make it? Had he been pressured to do so? Had he been promised a lenient sentence? These questions only caused more problems. Who had coerced Hammiltoun with threats and promises and why? What reason would William Mowat and Patrick Abernathy have in forcing Hammiltoun to make such an accusation? But if not them, then who? The only individuals left were Mowat of Fawside and Sir George. They also had the problem that Mowat of Fawside and Sir George remained the lead investigators in the Hammiltoun case. To remove them from the case implied they were guilty; to investigate them while the case was ongoing was risky. Again, the Privy Council were in an unenviable situation. After several discussions that lasted well into the night, they finally decided on the latter course and the vagabond's case was completed at the end of January.[27]

All charges against Lady Manderstoun were formally dropped on 2 February.[28] An investigation into the reasons behind the original accusation was instigated and Mowat of Fawside was arrested and put to the horn for lying about Hammiltoun's deposition against Lady Manderstoun. In July, however, after pressure from Mowat's friends, the Privy Council rescinded the order against him. William Mowat and Patrick Abernathy were quietly released and returned to work for Mowat of Fawside. In 1631, charges of fabricating confessions were brought against Mowat of Fawside in another witchcraft case. Found proven, he was arrested but managed again with help from his family to escape imprisonment. In late 1630, Sir George had to petition the Privy Council for protection against his creditors. He claimed the expenses he had incurred during the Hammiltoun case were a drain upon his purse.[29] He had previously owed some £14,000 to his father-in-law and money had been a constant issue between him and Lady Arnot. No charges were ever laid against him concerning his wife and Hammiltoun's confession.

In the original confession about Lady Manderstoun, Hammiltoun claimed to have introduced her to Auld Nick and that they had all had communal sex. He also claimed that they had taken part in a ritual using a dead fowl to bewitch Sir George to death. This had taken place in a barn on Sir George's land. What was the most damning was obvious. What was the most scandalous, however, was the idea of a lady of the nobility, who was of child-bearing age and could thus produce an heir, having intercourse with a vagabond. Innocent of the charges she might have been; whether she was innocent of the act was another matter.

It was never satisfactorily established who, if anyone, had coerced Hammiltoun into naming Lady Manderstoun. Had he been induced to name her, as some thought? Or was she indeed a witch and had lain with Hammiltoun to induce him to kill her husband? Hammiltoun's retraction came after the Privy Council had spoken to Mowat and Abernathy. Had the Haddington vagabond sensed how the wind had changed and altered his story accordingly?

The decisions of the Privy Council in this case were a balancing act between determining the truth and offending powerful members of the nobility. The decision not to interview Hammiltoun until after Mowat and Abernathy had been seen, contrary to normal practice, was never questioned. What can be gleaned from the records is that, at the time, at least two members of the Privy Council were related to the Arnot family.

On 10 November 1632, Lady Manderstoun scandalised Berwickshire once again by divorcing her husband.[30] It was said this was proof of her wickedness and ungodliness. It was also said that her husband was glad to be rid of her as of late he had not felt safe in his bed at night. Alexander Hammiltoun's fate remains unknown.

The main issue in the Hammiltoun/Manderstoun case was one of family honour. From the earliest medieval times in European culture, men of the nobility had three main functions which 'proved' their honour: to win in battle, to provide for their household and to produce sons. These functions had not lessened by the 17th century but had in most cases intensified and, as a result, those who could not perform such functions soon found their position in society under threat as they were judged to be lacking in male virility and honour. Each function, in turn, had consequences that affected all around them. To win in battle, or at least die in the attempt (the only honourable alternative), became increasingly difficult to undertake if there were no battles in which to participate. Jousting tournaments were developed to test the mettle and although most were undertaken with blunted lances, they could be dangerous. In 1559, in France, King Henry II died of wounds suffered in a tournament. The need for battle prowess required sons to undertake military training whether they wanted to or not. Sons who were physically impaired in any way or psychologically unsuited to military training were put under immense stress. To this day, male members of the British royal family are expected to hold some rank in the armed forces.

The second function of a noble was to provide for this household. This was much more than simply providing food and shelter for one's immediate family. A noble was responsible for the food, clothing, shelter, protection, education and, in some cases, taxes for family, household servants and any peasants that worked their land. Depending on the definition of family, this could encompass several dozen members. For the clans in the north of Scotland and the Border families, any member of the family no matter how distant had the right to ask for aid from the head of the family.

In addition to this, the higher the level of nobility, the more one was expected to entertain other members of the upper classes. This showed how much the noble was able to maintain his household but could and frequently did result in large debts that were seldom paid off but could be passed onto sons as part of their inheritance. Daughters were frequently married off to other families in lieu of a debt payment.

The final function of a nobleman was to produce sons. This was in part to ensure that land did not go out of the family but also to provide soldiers for whoever was the overlord of that noble – in the final instance, the King. As these sons would, however, marry the daughters of other nobles, there had to be an assurance they were the actual sons of their fathers. Herein lies the crux of the problem concerning Hammiltoun/Manderstoun. If a noblewoman lay with a commoner and became pregnant by him but passed the child off as the true son of her husband then the whole system came crashing down. Adultery with another noble was frowned upon but sexual intercourse with a peasant was unthinkable. The noble was cuckolded, the woman branded a whore, the child a bastard. The accusation that Hammiltoun had lain with Lady Manderstoun was the worst that could be levelled as a noble woman. If men 'proved' their honour by their ability to fight, provide and produce sons then women 'proved' theirs by their virginity on their wedding night and by the purity of their conduct. Women who produced sons for their husbands were publicly lauded and held up as an example of perfect womanhood; those who could not were shamed. Men who produced sons were virile, manly creatures; those who did not could blame their wives all they wanted but their lack of manhood was obvious to all.

The consequences of noble men being unable to fulfil their three noble functions could have far reaching effects. One of the most famous examples is Henry VIII of England. As a late medieval King, Henry VIII had to contend with the three noble functions but he also had the knowledge that his family's hold on the crown was both recent and contested by several other leading families in England. He also had to deal with the fact that he had never been expected to be King; that fate had been expected for his older brother, Arthur. By the time he became King, therefore, the expectations as to his conduct and subsequent psychological pressure on him was intense.

He was thwarted in his ambition to win a battle because England was not as war with anyone. To compensate, he spent a great deal of his time jousting and competing in tournaments. Providing for his household was also problematic as, until the dissolution of the monasteries, the royal exchequer was not wealthy. That left the final challenge: to produce a son. Politically, a son and heir would secure the dynasty, consolidating the right of the house of Tudor to aspire to the royal crown and prevent a return to the chaos of the Wars of the Roses. But more than that, a son would prove Henry was a man while those of his wives unable to produce a son paid the price. The other functions might prove honour but siring a son was also a matter for male pride above all. Henry may have died in 1547 but, in 1628 in Duns, that male pride still ran deep. Hammiltoun's dalliance with Lady Manderstoun, real or imagined, struck at that pride and undermined the trust that a nobleman's son was truly his.

6

Eyemouth, 1634

'the Devil be in your feet'

KNOWN LOCALLY AS a small fishing town but better known the length of Berwickshire as the haunt of smugglers and rogues, Eyemouth would, like other Borders towns, see many witches condemned to the flames in the 17th century. Coastal towns were frequently the site of witchcraft accusations as the dangers implicit in fishing and shipping along with the superstitions of fisherman all lent strength to the belief of malice when ships and lives were lost. In 1634, a trial was held that would expose the form of justice administered by the local Kirk and nobility and how, with some money, it was possible to challenge that justice. Eight women and men were arrested for witchcraft. At least four would be put to death and two more would commit suicide; one, Elizabeth Bathgate, would walk free after an acquittal in Edinburgh.

Elizabeth was a 57-year-old native of Eyemouth. She was married to a maltman (brewer), Alexander Pae, and as such was reasonably well off; the Bathgates were middling folk. In addition to working as a maltman, Alexander Pae was servant to Mr George Auchthertown (Ochterlony). Until the early 1630s, Elizabeth and Alexander had lived in relative peace with her neighbours. They had a trustworthy reputation and attended the Kirk on a Sunday. In 1631, this changed.

The charges against her seem to have arisen as a result of a series of disputes with several neighbours. George Sprot had borrowed some cloth from Elizabeth. After George had held onto the cloth for longer than Elizabeth had expected, she demanded its return while cursing him for his tardiness. A few days later she visited his house determined to get the cloth back. George was out and Elizabeth grew angry and allegedly nipped his son on the arm and then left,

leaving behind an egg. When he returned, George took the egg and
threw it at Elizabeth's house. Despite this, his son grew ill with an
egg-shaped lump on his body and then died. Elizabeth was also
alleged to have crippled another neighbour, William Donaldsoune,
with whom she had quarrelled, by calling out 'the Devil be in your
feet' when he ran from her. William had never been ill before but
was left limping and in pain for several months. She laid an illness
on the child of a third neighbour, John Gray. The child sickened
and lay ill for several weeks with an unnamed fever. This was due
to an argument she had with John who had turned his back on her.
She had a long-running feud with Margaret Home who had, on
numerous occasions, borrowed money from Elizabeth's husband.
Unfortunately, Margaret did not always repay the money promptly
and thus incurred Elizabeth's anger. Elizabeth cursed Margaret on
at least three separate occasions. These curses killed one horse, sent
another mad and killed an ox. Finally, she was accused of laying a
sickness on yet another neighbour, Steven Allan, after an argument
that had grown heated.[31]

While the Kirk elders led by the minister, John Hume, were
preparing to deal with these matters, a local mill caught fire and
suspicion fell on Elizabeth. The Kirk was convinced and the local
sheriff interrogated several local suspects. Several names were given
to the authorities including that of Elizabeth. While the arguments
with her neighbours and the laying of illness was enough for the
secular authorities, what was serious in the eyes of the Kirk were
the accusations that were laid against her of dealing with the Devil.
Two local men swore they had seen her talking to a man in fine
green clothes they thought was Auld Nick. Elizabeth was dressed
only in her sark (petticoat) at the time and when they had spoken
to her, she had ignored them and one man told the other of her bad
reputation saying 'her name is not lucky'.[32] This was followed by
an accusation that Auld Nick had given her a horseshoe, which she
had buried at his instruction and with the understanding that if she
did as he bade she would never want for money. She was named by
several other suspected witches as having been with them at a meeting with the Devil presiding and later when they had destroyed a
mill. They also named her as one of the group that had sunk George
Hurdie's boat. One of the witches, William Mearns, described as a

'notorious warlock',[33] stated that she was a witch and had been at several witch assemblies at which the Devil had presided. A second witch, Margaret Ballanie, also named Elizabeth calling her a 'sicker witch' [34] than herself.

While this was a longer than usual list of complaints, it was the normal litany of offences against witches. In 1633, papers were lodged against Alison Wilson, Agnes Wilson, Elspeth Wilson, William Mearns, Margaret Ballanie in Aytoun, Patrick Smith, Jennet Williamson and Elizabeth Bathgate. All were rounded up by the baillie and his men and incarcerated. For some reason that remains unclear, Elizabeth Bathgate was sent to the tolbooth in Duns while the others were all incarcerated in Eyemouth. It may be that she was considered more dangerous than the others and had to be separated from them or it could have been a more prosaic reason. Elizabeth was the last to be arrested so there may simply not have been sufficient room left in Eyemouth gaol.

Whatever the reason, she did not take too kindly to her imprisonment and, on 16 December 1633, she lodged a complaint with the Privy Council against Sir Patrick Hume of Ayton and Mr John Hume, minister of Eyemouth, for illegally imprisoning her on a charge of witchcraft. Elizabeth Bathgate was to prove no helpless victim. This was the first of four complaints she made to the Privy Council. Strength of character such as this was surely needed to fight an accusation of witchcraft. However, it could prove to be a handicap as evidence of a quarrelsome nature was a charge levelled at many women accused of being witches.

Most accused witches were abandoned by friends and family and sent their time awaiting trial sitting in a filthy cell on a semi-starvation diet. Elizabeth had managed, somehow, to get someone to visit her, write down a complaint and get it sent up to Edinburgh to the Privy Council on four different occasions. It is not clear how she knew to write to the Privy Council or even that she had the right to do so but it would appear that Elizabeth had not been entirely abandoned her family.

On 9 January 1634, Elizabeth complained again about her false imprisonment. On 11 February, she was moved to Edinburgh Tolbooth in preparation for her trial. The pre-trial preparations had taken longer than expected and, again on 11 February, Elizabeth complained about this and the financial hardship that maintaining her in prison was costing her family. On 27 February, she lodged her final complaint that the witness depositions that had been taken outwith her presence, and not in a court of justice, were going to be offered into evidence in her trial. This final complaint, although in Elizabeth's name, saw the use of legal language and understanding of the court system and so probably emanated from her legal team. Somehow Elizabeth had found an advocate to defend her. The statements were disallowed unless the deposers came to Edinburgh to ratify them. Elizabeth then petitioned for release from prison pending the actual trial. She asked for a warrant to remain in Edinburgh which was granted. She was released from the tolbooth in Edinburgh on 11 March.[35]

On 4 of June 1634, the Lord Advocate and Sir Patrick Hume brought their case against Elizabeth in Edinburgh. Eighteen different counts were laid against her and, as at least two other named witches had 'delated' or named her as a witch, her chances were not good. However, Elizabeth did have a strong defence team that consisted of Robert Burnet, defence advocate; Laurence MacGill, defence advocate; David Prymrois, defence advocate; and her husband Alexander Pae who had stood by her.

The full charges against Elizabeth were: murder of George Sprot's child by nipping and using an enchanted egg; causing George Sprot to become poor; crippling William Donaldson; laying a sickness on John Gray's bairn; killing Margaret Homes' horse; killing Margaret Homes' ox; making Margaret Homes' horse mad; damaging George Auchterlonie's barn; conjuring and running widdershins on the mill; talking to the Devil in her shift; being delated a witch by Margaret Ballanie; burning the mill at Eyemouth with other witches; burying a horseshoe Auld Nick had given her; being delated a witch by William Mearns, a warlock; sinking George Huldie's ship with other witches and, after being confronted by these other witches, being delated by them.

The charges were both serious and numerous and her defence team set about having as many of the charges as possible dropped before the trial began. They started on the charge of having sunk George Hurdie's ship. This was a serious charge, not least because it would raise memories in many of the North Berwick witches who

had tried to drown the King by raising a storm to sink his ship in
1590. The advocates used sophisticated arguments to ridicule these
charges, calling them dreams and idle visions rather than a serious
criminal charge. They stated that the indictment, and by implication
the authorities in Eyemouth, had not even had the wit to dream up
a storm raising like the North Berwick witches. The Edinburgh court
would smirk at the stupidity of their country cousins down in the
Borders. The advocates continued in the same vein: why not have
Elizabeth and the other witches fly round the ship like crows? This was
an especially clever move. There are very few instances of accusations
of Scottish witches flying. It was considered a delusion in Scotland,
although interestingly it was a relatively common accusation on the
continent. These lawyers were learned in both law and European tradition. Pandering to the intellect and egos of the Edinburgh courts,
they mocked the charges to great effect.

The defence advocates then turned to some of the lesser offences,
managing to have the charges of making George Sprot poor and
causing Margaret Homes' horse to go mad dropped from the dittay
(legal charge). Again, they used ridicule to good effect. Cause and
effect could no more be definitively linked than if a child chased a
chicken that stopped laying eggs a week later. After this brief inter-
lude, they moved onto more serious matters. The charge of conjuration and running widdershins was also thrown out. These charges
depended on the statements of known witches, Margaret Ballanie
and William Mearns. Were not witches liars? So their statements
could not be relied upon. This was important as both actions were
strong indicators of witchcraft with a diabolical element. The next
two charges were of burying the horseshoe given to her by Auld
Nick and of having been seen by two men talking to the Devil in her
shift. Both of these charges were also thrown out as based on gossip.
Her defence team then moved on to the two most serious charges:
that she had been delated by the witches Margaret Ballanie and
William Mearns. They managed to argue that these charges were
not relevant as the statements of delation had been taken after the
other charges were listed; those charges that had just been dropped.
Ballanie and Mearns had only delated Elizabeth after being told
what charges she faced. As these charges had now been dropped,
Ballanie and Mearns should never have been asked if Elizabeth was

a witch. The delations were dropped from the indictment against her. This was a major victory. To be delated by another witch was an almost certain death sentence. Moreover, this undermined the last remaining charges, including those of the two murders. Her advocates argued simply: if she had had no contact with the Devil and was not a witch as the Crown had originally stated then how, and why, would she murder?

The jury was of a similar mind. Elizabeth Bathgate was acquitted of all charges against her. The other witches were not so lucky. Patrick Smith was found dead in his cell in Eyemouth gaol, probably a result of his treatment while there. Worse was to come. William Mearns had managed to escape from gaol and during the escape found enough rope to hang himself. It was said that he 'put hands on himself at the devill's instigation'. Both bodies were committed to unhallowed ground. Tales were muttered around Eyemouth about guards that left open doors and escaping prisoners that 'found' rope. Mr Hume the minister preached from his pulpit about how idle gossip could be used by the Devil to ensnare the stupid and the talk died down. Margaret Ballanie, Alison Wilson, Agnes Wilson and Elspeth Wilson were all found guilty of witchcraft and legally worriet before their bodies were burned.[36]

So why was Elizabeth acquitted? Elizabeth Bathgate lodged four complaints before and during her trial. While this was not unknown, it was generally dismissed unless there was gross illegality going on. In Elizabeth's case, the complaints were upheld to the extent that Sir Patrick Hume was barred from giving evidence due to his 'gross prejudice' against her. Sir Patrick may have been a knight of the realm but Elizabeth stood firm. While the prosecution team was led by the local aristocracy and numbered 11 prosecutors, investigators and expert witnesses, Elizabeth, wife of a maltman, managed to afford to muster a defence team of three defence advocates so influential that they managed to have the trial transferred to Edinburgh where she would not face a local jury that knew her. Was her defence team brilliant, was the prosecution team poor or was something else going on? Why was Sir Patrick so prejudiced against her? What was his relation to the minister John Hume, so keen to find witches in his parish? And why was she acquitted when the others were found guilty?

Sir Patrick's hatred of Elizabeth could have a number of reasons but for it to have been so strong as to warrant censure from the Privy Council it must have had a good cause, at least in Sir Patrick's mind. As a member of the local nobility, he would have been extremely influential during the trial proceedings and this is probably why the defence team fought to have the trial moved to Edinburgh where his influence would be lessened.

Elizabeth's defence team persuaded the authorities to move the trial. They outlined Sir Patrick's malice towards Elizabeth. At some point the pair had met over some business and Elizabeth had been less than deferential in their dealings. The advocates further stated that Sir Patrick was cousin to John Hume the minister and that each had 'great trust' in the judgement of the other, one anxious to find witches, the other to put a maltman's wife in her place. The defence team then detailed the fact that witness depositions had been taken outwith her presence, and not in a court of justice. They also managed to get some of these statements disallowed as the deposers had not come to Edinburgh to ratify them. During the actual trial they used legal arguments to defeat several of the arguments against her. The advocates demanded the legal niceties were adhered to in accordance with the law. In short, Elizabeth's team, did their job. The fact that the other accused witches, tried in Eyemouth, were found guilty merely adds to this. Had they had access to advocates, they too might have been acquitted. The case against Elizabeth and her co-accused was quite simply not strong enough but in Eyemouth, with Sir Patrick presiding, convictions were a foregone conclusion.

The prosecution team consisted of Sir Patrick Hume (complaint of false imprisonment against him upheld by the Privy Council); George Hume, Minister of Aytoun and another cousin of Sir Patrick (deprived of his ministry in 1650 after an unspecified complaint about his behaviour and had a complaint of false imprisonment against him upheld by the Privy Council); John Hume, minister of Eyemouth (complaint of false imprisonment against him upheld by the Privy Council); Sir Thomas Hope of Craighall, Knight Baronet; Sir Thomas Hope of Craighall, son of Sir Thomas Hope, Knight Baronet; Issobel Ker, Lady Ayton wife of Sir Patrick; George Auchhthertown, Alexander Pae's employer; Christopher Knowles, minister at Coldingham (dismissed for adultery in 1641); Sir John Ramsay of Edington; Mark Hume, another Hume family member; John Oliphant; and Isobel Young.

This case is not a typical witchcraft trial. The number of high-status individuals involved indicates that something more than a local accusation lay at the root of it. The extreme prejudice of Sir Patrick extended to using his wife, Lady Ayton, as the main expert witness against Elizabeth. Why were the local nobility so keen to secure her conviction and probable execution? The lack of deference shown by Elizabeth to Sir Patrick was, no doubt, galling to his pride but was it a sufficient reason for an entire trial involving 11 other prosecutors?

The small coves around Eyemouth had long been a favoured landing place for goods that wanted to escape the eye of the excise man (taxman). As the wife of a maltman and active in his business, Elizabeth would have been aware of the movement of goods in and out of the town. Her husband's employment as a servant would also have given them access to information about the local nobility's business dealings. Was the case brought against Elizabeth tainted by these local concerns? Sir Patrick was the son of Sir Patrick Hume, the Scottish courtier and makar. Although highly talented, on his death in 1609, Sir Patrick Hume the elder left his son only his estates and some outstanding debts. With little of his father's talent or easy wit, the younger Sir Patrick spent less time at court and more time on his estates which he resolved to expand. Between 1609 and 1648, when he died, Sir Patrick bought up several parcels of land around his estates, increased the quality and quantity of his cattle and generally improved the value of his land. Nowhere in the records, however, can it be seen where he raised the capital for these improvements.

It is also curious to note that Elizabeth Bathgate's defence team comprised three advocates. Although the Bathgates were middling folk, the costs of three defence advocates and a trial was an expensive burden that should have been out of their reach, especially given Elizabeth's complaint about the costs of the trial. However, she had afforded the use of advocates and removal of the trial to Edinburgh saved her life. The evidence that convicted Margaret Ballanie, Alison Wilson, Agnes Wilson, Elspeth Wilson, Jennet Williamson and Patrick Smith was the same as the evidence that acquitted Elizabeth Bathgate. No sentence was ever brought against Sir Patrick for the false imprisonment of Elizabeth Bathgate.

The Scottish Kirk had no doubt that witches existed. All the most learned church men and philosophers of western Europe had written numerous books on the subject. Even King James VI himself had written his great treatise *Daemonologie* on the subject after the incident when the witches of North Berwick had raised a storm to try and drown him and his new bride in 1590. The religious wars that had ravaged Europe in the wake of the Reformation had thrown the world into turmoil. While Princes and emperors turned to the sword to protect their territories and root out heretics, church men and philosophers sought the path of learning to offer certainty and security in troubled times. Heretics lurked round every corner and the Devil, his witches and their wicked arts threatened faith and faithful alike. While the Reformation may have split mother church, learned manuscripts on witchcraft were eagerly sought by all no matter the faith of the author. All Christendom was in peril and the question was how to bring witches swiftly and securely to justice.

Between the mid-15th and mid-17th centuries, several major manuscripts and treatises were written to help churchmen in their never-ending battle against heretics and witches. While there were a few writers that disputed the existence of both witches and witchcraft, they were overwhelmingly in the minority. Most disputed the existence of witches on the grounds that the Devil would not use women for his diabolical purposes as they were too stupid to be of much use. The vast majority of manuscripts, taking the existence of witches as self-evident, outlined in great detail how to identify and prosecute those witches. Written by theologians, lawyers and philosophers, it was these manuscripts that laid the basis of the proofs acceptable to courts throughout Europe.

The Scottish courts recognised four proofs of an individual being a witch: having a history of bad behaviour or of having committed evils acts; being named witch by another witch, or 'delated' as it was known in the Scottish courts; confessing to being a witch and being found with the Devil's mark[37] on the body. An initial accusation of having committed an act of witchcraft would usually trigger an investigation: a 'Commission to try a witch'. The Commission looked to find one or more of the four proofs of witchcraft. In most cases they found their proof. Despite the chaos that surrounded them and their belief in the Devil's intention to attack the Kirk, most local clergy were aware of how easily an accusation could arise. Wild accusations with no corroborating proof were quickly dismissed. In most cases where the individuals concerned were known to the minister, no Commission was sought and the initial accusation was dismissed. In all other cases, a Commission would quickly uncover proof.

The first and most easily found 'proof' was a bad reputation. This could be built up over a number of years and was a dangerous attribute to develop especially in a small community. This was more than just being disliked in an area; it was where an individual had a history of suspicious behaviour or of practising witchcraft. Many of those arrested had been performing witchcraft for many years often for friends or neighbours perhaps by helping find lost property or curing sickness with charms and chants. The individual may even have had a previous conviction for witchcraft. Occasionally a local presbytery would, if someone was found guilty, merely excommunicate them from the Kirk or, if the offence was relatively minor, simply admonish them. This had been the general method of punishment in previous centuries. However, as the years went on, a reputation might grow worse and instead of curing illness the individual might be suspected of causing illness.

The court records give sad testimony to this aspect of 'proof' and how mundane and easily it could be attained. Arguing with your neighbours or even your husband was always suspect and as much of life then was public – the marketplace, the farm, the town square – a family squabble could all too easily be seen and heard. Complaining about services or goods was also a minefield. An assertion that the butter you had bought had been spoiled or the milk watered could, over time, make your name as a 'quarrelsome' person. Once labelled 'quarrelsome', every word spoken in haste or anger could then add to the reputation.

And then there were two situations that hugely affected an individual's reputation: non-attendance at the Kirk and the death of a relative or neighbour. Unless ill, and severely so, not going to the Kirk on Sunday was unthinkable. Human memory is an imperfect tool so that an incident of non-attendance could be remembered and commented upon long after the cause of it was forgotten. Death of a relative or neighbour also raised suspicion. A man who lost his wife in childbirth was to be pitied while a woman who lost her husband was to be avoided. Husbands who died of natural causes, unless very old, were assumed to have been bewitched to death. Accidental death raised the suspicion that the wife had 'caused' the accident. And death after an illness of a relatively fit healthy male could have been the result of poison. These fears extended out to other relatives, friends and neighbours. As most of those who cared for the sick were women, any unusual death could result in suspicion and damage to their reputation.

Many trial records note a bad reputation going back over ten and even 20 years. Neighbours and ministers who reported on the suspect were seldom questioned as to the veracity of their statements and local gossip became enshrined as proof once recorded by court clerks.

Of those named in the trial records existing in Scotland, 7 per cent were below the age of 20; 8 per cent were between 20 and 30; 22 per cent were between 30 and 40; 22 per cent were between 40 and 50; and 38 per cent were over 50. A history of 'witch' behaviour over many years would build up until a final or more severe charge was laid and an arrest made. Those under the age of 20 tended to be the sons, and more frequently, daughters of known witches. Reputation also suffered from the changing attitudes of society and Kirk. Being known as a witch in 1580 would bring the disapproval and condemnation of the Kirk; by 1600 the same, possibly trivial, offences were viewed more seriously and dealt with more harshly. Previous arguments over crops or food which had been relatively innocent thus developed more sinister overtones. Stories of illnesses brought on after an argument or good fortune turning to bad would more readily be attributed to an act of witchcraft and taken by the courts as fact.

Another aspect of the heightened times and fears developed whereby a reputation could, unfortunately, be inherited. A mother, and in some cases a grandmother, who had previously had a reputation as a witch could result in a daughter being arrested, the logic being that, had the daughter been a good Christian, she would have reported the mother as a witch. If no report was forthcoming then the daughter, or son, must be a witch as well. Several court records list mother and daughters as co-accused.

The second 'proof' of being a witch was if a suspected or known witch named or 'delated' another individual. Even more than a bad reputation this was considered strong proof of witch-craft. Those named by another witch rarely escaped a guilty verdict. Interrogations of suspected witches always included questioning about accomplices in the particular crime under investigation or of any other known witches. Interrogators would press hard on this point eager to round up all the guilty parties in the area. Suspects would frequently be asked who had inducted them into witchcraft eg their mother or close relative, who had led them to dance with the Devil. It was common for a woman and her daughters to be arrested together and pressed to name each other as witches. Young women were often persuaded to name those who had inducted them into witchcraft with promises of more lenient treatment. Such promises were seldom kept. Certain young witches were occasionally imprisoned while their older co-accused was executed. However, this lenient treatment was never repeated and on release from gaol the individual had a ready-made bad reputation which laid them open to future accusations in the future.

It was commonly believed that witches were inducted into a pact with the Devil when others were present as witnesses and questioning would frequently follow this line of reasoning. A witch would be asked what other witches were present when they met the Devil. Witches were also thought to congregate, even if the Devil was not present, to carry out their witchcraft. This derived from beliefs about women's inferiority. Servants of the Devil they might be but they were still weak and needed to meet together to be able to perform their magic. No such stricture was laid upon warlocks. As a result, meetings with other women in the evening or at night, even if for no more sinister reason than to pass the time of day, would be suspect. Even where witches worked alone it was thought that one witch could recognise another even if they were strangers and so pressure was brought to bear to name others.

The third proof of witchcraft and the one the interrogators always sought was a formal confession of being a witch. This usually took the form of a confession of meeting the Devil either alone or in the company of other witches. The witch would then enter into a pact with Auld Nick and thus reject Christ. The form of the pact and how easily they had entered into it was important. The Kirk strove to prove the Devil was false and a liar and so the detail of what he had promised the witch and, hopefully, then failed to deliver was recorded not just to gain proof of witchcraft but also as an edification to others as to the true and deceitful nature of the Devil.

The women frequently talked of having had sex with Auld Nick and again detail was sought. Descriptions of how unnatural he was and how unlike a man were important points for the Kirk. It was believed that the Devil's penis was cold and great prominence would be given to this in the evidence presented to the courts. Sex with the Devil was a blasphemous form of adultery, even for those who were unmarried as all sex outside marriage was an adulterous sin. Sex within marriage was only allowed for the purposes of creating children and was forbidden on the several holy days that littered the year. After confessing to their pact with the Devil, the witch would then go on to list what they had done as a witch: laying on of sickness, ruining food or causing impotence in men. In short, they were expected to give a list of grievances against themselves usually far exceeding the initial charges that had been laid.

Confession was always sought by the Kirk and those who did not confess were almost always assumed to be stubborn liars rather than innocent. As the individual had probably already been named by another witch and had a reputation as a witch, to deny it was deemed impudent arrogance. The suspect had been named and was a known witch, how dare they refuse to confess when confronted by the Kirk with their own guilt? By not confessing, the witch was challenging the authority of the local Kirk that had brought the charges against her. She was as good as calling the local minister and elders liars. Such behaviour, which was noted and used within the trial, could only come from a witch. And that witch had to be made to confess to prove God's power. Kirk elders would make it a point of pride to boast that they had brought their witches to confession, while those unable to do similar would keep quiet.

As the century wore on, however, this zeal to bring witches to confession would lead to many of the excesses of torture and ill treatment. Ministers would not only look to nearby parishes for comparisons but also further afield and local pride became inflated when the large number of witches caught and brought to confession in the Borders was noted. The Devil always the attacked the most godly, so the more witches caught and made to confess proved the godliness of the Border's Presbyteries compared to other areas. A witch's confession to a compact with Auld Nick proved the godliness of the community.

As the Kirk strove to gain more confessions, so more confessions were given. In the 16th century, witch trials were a rarity and confessions seldom forthcoming. In the 17th century, with chaos all around them and a zealous Kirk convinced of its own righteousness, those accused of witchcraft confessed in higher numbers. Confessions became more frequent as the number of accused rose, although it must be noted that the greater number of those accused still refused to confess until compelled by torture. It is also true that some accused still did not confess even after torture.

The fourth and final proof was the existence of the Devil's mark. One of the major points of debate among scholars of the time was whether or not witches could act independently of the Devil. This was a serious matter. Could witches, for the most part women, commit evil acts? To admit this was to afford them a power not natural to women. While the malice and evil that lurked in witches and women was not denied, how this was harnessed by Auld Nick and ultimately allowed by God was a theological puzzle. In the Calvinist Kirk, the understanding, however, was much clearer: under the doctrine of predestination, the witches were foreordained to everlasting punishment as the handmaidens of the Devil and would be proved so to be.

It was believed that the Devil would mark his followers to seal their pact with him in a parody of Christian baptism. As the sign of the cross was made on the skin during a baptism, so he too would mark his followers. This Devil's mark was found by pricking or 'brodding' the accused witch with a steel pin or bodkin. Brodding was usually carried out where a suspected witch refused to confess and could often result in both finding the Devil's mark and a confession. Brodding was not considered torture but was merely part of the normal interrogation procedure.

With one or more of these 'proofs' in place, the witch could now be brought to trial.

7

Stow, 1649

'ane great syckness'

WITCHCRAFT WAS NOT confined to the larger Border towns and in 1630, the village of Stow imposed a tax of £2 on each plough in the parish to maintain warded witches. In its day, this was a large tax and, in an area totally dependent of farming, would have been a considerable burden to bear. So why was it imposed? Was Stow of Wedale so full of witches that they cost so much to keep until trial, or was the tax needed to pay for the trials of all these witches? Possibly both factors came into play. There is no record, however, of any complaints anent the tax perhaps indicating just how seriously the threat of witchcraft was taken. In such an agriculturally dependent area it was surely better to pay £2 towards the detection and prosecution of a witch than to have the harvest fail due to witchcraft. Nineteen years later, in 1649, the tax was to be put to good use.

The village of Stow, sitting alongside the Gala water, was an old settlement. It had been a sacred place since before Christianity, probably developing around the spring that was later developed into the lady's well and associated chapel. Pre-Christian pagan religions saw water as a sacred entity and a medium for communing with spirits. With the coming of Christianity to southern Scotland, sometime in the 6th century, Stow became associated with the Virgin Mary. In 846 AD, the Welsh monk Nennius wrote about King Arthur who had received a vision before the battle of Guinnon, in which the Virgin Mary promised victory to a Christian champion.[38] Arthur won the battle and, according to local legend, built a chapel just south of Stow in Mary's honour beside the existing well of spring water. By 635 AD, Stow church was known as a site of sanctuary to the north of Melrose that was associated with the Virgin. Monks from the borders abbeys at Melrose and Kelso were familiar with the prayer related to Our Lady of Wedale; 'O Mary, tender-fair, gentle-fair, loving-fair, Mary beloved! Mother of the white lamb! Our Lady of Wedale, pray for us!' [39] The village of Stow grew up half a mile to the north of the holy chapel and well and in 1242, Bishop David de Bernham of St Andrews consecrated the village church of St Mary which replaced the original chapel. After the Reformation, the church converted to Protestantism and the tradition of pilgrimage to the well stopped.

Despite this long tradition of religious worship, by the 17th century, Stow village was little more than a straggle of cottages clustered round the church with outlying farms. Its inhabitants varied between the few well-off famers, the majority who were poor but not destitute, mostly farm labourers, and the few village indigents that scratched an existence during the spring and summer and survived the autumn and winter on the charity of their neighbours. Farming dominated the village with a mixture of sheep and kye. Although blessed with good water and grazing, this good fortune had still seen the village suffer like the rest of the Borders when famine struck and plague crossed the valleys. They had suffered in 1644 as the harvest had failed and both people and animals had starved to death in that winter. A small village they could scarce afford to lose labour or livestock and the return of famine in 1648 had been a severe blow. The spring of 1649 had, therefore, been a welcome relief as the weather had seen a good number of calves born and crops planted for the coming year spared any sudden late frost. Everything seemed set fair when suddenly kye started to sicken and die. No other areas seemed to be affected. Healthy fat kye were seen munching contentedly on the Lauder side of the moor; it was only Stow that appeared to have a problem.

There could be only one explanation for these troubles and the word was out: witch. The village may have forgotten the origins and old religious traditions of Stow; the minister had not. Villagers that had started out as pagan worshippers and, worse still, worshipped as Catholics for around 1,000 years were not to be trusted. It was perfectly believable that Stow would have a witch.

The name Isobel Thompson was soon on everyone's lips and once mentioned to the minister, John Cleland, and the elders, the investigation began. A young man from Lauder was also named and quickly brought to book. Brought before the elders, he quickly confessed to being a warlock and named Isobel as his accomplice. She had, he claimed, seduced the man over several nights and initiated him into witchcraft. Isobel was arrested and the two were locked up in the cellar of the baillie's house. The Stow elders wrote to the Privy Council for a Commission and a rider and horse found to take the request up to Edinburgh, paid for from the plough tax. The legal Commission was quickly received and the formal investigation got underway.[40]

Isobel was in serious trouble, 'delated' as a witch by an accused witch was one of the four main proofs of witchcraft and more was to come. Unmarried, Isobel lived alone and did not appear to have had any financial support. But what she did have was a sharp tongue, an unfortunate inability to keep her temper and a reputation as a 'quarrelsome dame'.[41] There had been no hesitation or demur when her name was raised. By the time she was brought before the elders, her reputation had been thoroughly examined and found wanting. Old arguments and half remembered disagreements had been brought to the attention of the elders. Ill repute was being added to being delated and more and more accusations were raised.

Unbowed by the wrath of Mr Cleland and denying everything put to her, Isobel refused to confess. Hard questioning then turned to hard walking as the baillie's men were instructed to walk her until she came to her senses. The walking went on long into the night and eventually a confession of sorts was extracted. Isobel had confessed to witchcraft but had also named another Margaret Dunholme. Margaret was also from Stow and also unmarried. She was soon arrested and joined Isobel and the Lauder man in the baillie's cellar. Further questioning was undertaken and further inquiries in the village.

The final list of charges laid against the three were possibly as bad as they could be in a rural community, short of murder, and centred round the ruining of one local farmer by putting 'ane great syckness on his kye'.[42] Within the week his cattle had started to sicken and die and Isobel and the others were identified as the cause. In a rural community, the death of livestock for some could meant the difference between eating and starvation, so laying illness on livestock was recognised for its severity.

Stow was so small that magistrates and a clerk for the trial had to be sought from elsewhere and this took time. Unluckily for Isobel, Margaret and their male co-accused who were facing weeks incarcerated in an airless cellar awaiting trial, the summer was proving to be hot and sticky. And while statements had to be been taken and a jury found and sworn in, hands were needed in the fields. Who had time to sit in a courtroom? However, finally in the late summer the trial began.

The charges of witchcraft were formally laid: denial of God, using witchcraft to sicken and kill kye, using witchcraft to ruin crops. All three had, under questioning and walking, confessed and these confessions were read out. The denial of God and the turning to the Devil's ways was, in the eyes of the Kirk, the major crime. The Minister reminded the three accused of the crisis that was facing the land as the godless strove to overthrow the normal order. For a farming community, the more life-threatening crime was the death of livestock. The local jury delivered the verdict – guilty – and the sentence – to be worriet and then burned to death – followed immediately. The Kirk elders congratulated each other. Three more of the Devil's followers would be consigned to the flames. The righteous had triumphed and all would see that evil was always found out. The village breathed a collective sigh of relief; life could get back to normal.

But the respite was brief. The ungodly were not finished with Stow yet. While the Kirk prepared for the execution of Isobel, Margaret and the Lauder man, muttered suspicions were again heard in the village. The elders may have been preparing to dispatch these three witches to hell fire but more witches were abroad that summer. The trial had fixed everyone's attention, but what of the rest of the happenings in the village? Some of the kye were still ill; and the hot dry summer was becoming too hot, too dry. The river was low and the lack of rain was starting to see crops shrivelling in the fields. Those kye not sick were to be found each day in the river attempting to keep cool. Three more names started to be muttered and the previous relief disappeared like a morning mist. James Henrison, Marion Henrison and Jonet Henrison, husband, wife and possibly sister, were named witches.

15th century engraving, Pope Innocent VIII.

John Knox statue in courtyard of New College, Edinburgh. © Mary W. Craig

17th century woodcut, horned Devil with dancers.

17th century woodcut, two witches casting a spell for bad weather.

17th century woodcut, three witches with their familiars.

17th century woodcut, witches raising a storm to sink a ship.

17th century woodcut,
witch flying on a goat.

17th century woodcut, male witches
pledging themselves to the Devil.

17th century woodcut,
a Witches' Sabbath.

17th century woodcut, old witch with crow.

18th century woodcut, witches dancing with devils. © Wellcome Collection

18th century woodcut, woman meeting a black-faced witch with a giant beast. © Wellcome Collection

Woman abandoning baby. © Rhiannon Hunt

Witch burning. © Rhiannon Hunt

John Kincaid, from contemporary records.
© Rhiannon Hunt

Tor Hill, Peebles. One of the sites where the Peebles' witches met. © Mike and Jessica Troughton

Maxtoun Farmland. Typical rural lanscape of the time where the Melrose witches may have met. © Mike and Jessica Troughton

Abbotsford Farmland. Typical rural landscape of the time where Janet Armstrong may have worked as a 'healer'. © Mike and Jessica Troughton

Halliwell's Close, Selkirk. Typical street of the time where Meg Lawson might have been dragged to her execution. © Mike and Jessica Troughton

Ettrick and Yarrow landscape. The areas where witches' babies were abandoned. © Mike and Jessica Troughton

Stow Auld Kirk. Where the minster of Stow preached against witches. © Mike and Jessica Troughton

Stow Bridge. The site of the Stow witch executions. © Mike and Jessica Troughton

Lauder moor. The moor leading from Stow to Lauder which Hob Grieve crossed to meet the Devil. © Mike and Jessica Troughton

Reputations were once again under investigation. Vague suspicions were shared but while they could not be ignored, the three, although suspect, had not been delated and so further proof was needed. The main charge against James Henrison was that he had once used a charm he had got from Isobel Thompson to heal a broken arm.[43] The elders met and sat long into the night. Convinced of the guilt of the three Henrisons but aware of the lack of any real evidence against them, the elders sent for John Kincaid.

In the meantime, the three Henrisons were arrested and locked in the Kirk. It was not thought fit to allow them to be locked in with the three convicted witches. With three convicted witches in the baillie's cellar, and three more suspected witches in the Kirk, more men were needed to guard them. Men were needed for the building of the execution pyre for the original three but also for walking and watching the Henrisons. And a new jury would have to be sworn in once the new trial began. This time everyone would be called on to do their duty.

The next morning saw James, Jonet and Marion standing before the foremost witch brodder in Scotland. Word had spread round the village: Kincaid was here. A crowd gathered. Three witches to be executed, three more suspected, and the great John Kincaid in the village. The murmurs grew. The elders of Stow knew their flock and knew what could happen when fear gave way to panic, a firm hand was needed. They had met with Kincaid that morning and explained their predicament. This was a sore test for the elders but they were determined not to be found wanting in their duty. They would root out the Devil and all his works. Kincaid listened carefully to their instructions. His experience in these matters was well known and his counsel to the elders duly noted. They were decided: he was to be given a free rein.

James, Jonet and Marion were brought before Kincaid and the elders flanked on either side by the baillie's men. Questioned as to whether any of them were witches, all three denied the charge. Kincaid put to work. James was stripped naked and shaved and made to stand before Kincaid. The brodder examined James' body for any blemish or spot that might be the Devil's mark. As James was restrained by the baillie's men, Kincaid brodded him in several places about the neck and shoulders. This involved pushing a two- or three-inch steel pin or bodkin into the person's body. The first few attempts drew blood but eventually a small insensitive spot that did not bleed was found. The Devil's mark was discovered. This was duly recorded and James was returned to the Kirk. The elders turned to Jonet, who had seen the treatment of her brother, and asked her to confess; but still she denied the charge. She was stripped and shaved and again brodded with the bodkin until the Devil's mark was also found on her. Lastly, Marion was brought forward. Another denial, another brodding and another Devil's mark found and noted. The elders were satisfied, they had their evidence. Kincaid was paid six pounds Scots for the brodding, with a further three pounds paid by the Stow parish from the plough tax for meat and drink for Kincaid and his servant.

Jonet, Marion and James' trial began the next day. Witness statements had been taken and the jury sworn in. The sole charge against them was that of being witches. No specific accusations of casting spells or causing harm had been laid. The main evidence against them was the discovery of the Devil's mark, which was taken as unshakeable proof of their guilt. The jury took barely five minutes to declare all three guilty and the Commissioners sentenced them to death.

The next day, Isobel, Margaret and the young Lauder man were taken out of the baillie's cellar, led out to the edge of the Gala water and then worriet and burned on the pyre. One week later, Jonet, Marion and James followed them. Note has been made that one James Henrison was an indweller of Stow in 1650 and it has been suggested that James may have somehow escaped execution. While it is possible that as a man James was spared but as he was sentenced to death that is unlikely. If he were to be treated more leniently than the women, that would have happened at the trial with the possibility of a reduced sentence of excommunication and exile from the village. There are a few cases where men have been granted a stay of execution while they gather evidence to appeal their sentence. However, this is also unlikely in this case as James had the Devil's mark on him, one of the definite proofs of witchcraft and found by the foremost witch brodder in Scotland. What is more likely is that the James Henrison of 1650 was a son or some other relative of the man executed in 1649.

One of the curious elements of the Stow witch trials is the 'Lauder lad', as he came to be known. None of the trial records name him, although both Isobel and Margaret are clearly identified. In some of the witch trial records, the accused are merely listed as 'several witches' or 'four witches' but it is rare, although not unknown, for some of the individuals in a case to be named and others to remain anonymous. In these cases, most of those that remain anonymous are men. This usually happened when a family had enough money or influence to persuade the local clerk to omit their relative's names. A father or husband might well be mixed up in witchcraft but the family could still try to salvage something from the disaster if the family name was not recorded. And while locals might well know the name, trading further afield in the likes of Melrose or Selkirk might just be possible. A few of the arrest warrants held in the archives show where the names of male suspects have been scored out.

Witch hunting was a serious and godly business and those involved did so for religious reasons. The uncovering and prosecution of witches was a duty in which everyone in a parish was expected to participate. However, there were those possessed of a special skill in detecting witches and these were the witch brodders. There were around ten witch brodders in Scotland and these individuals, all men, would travel round the country, for a fee, aiding interrogations and giving evidence to Commissions.

The belief that, in becoming a witch, the woman or man had denied their baptism and made a pact with Auld Nick was of grave concern. Again, the great theologians and philosophers took up their pens to write on the matter. Debate was engaged as to the size and location of marks, what was their level of sensation, whether they would draw blood if pricked and even whether or not every witch was marked by the Devil.

The Devil's mark was generally, though not always, found on the shoulder. It could also be found on the head or neck or, less commonly in Scotland, on other parts of the body. The accused witch's head would be shaved and then the shoulder, head and neck searched for the mark. If not found then the whole body would be shaved and searched. The mark itself might be anything, a small mole or freckle, a birthmark or a wart and could be large

or small. Brodding a mark once it had been found involved insert-
ing a long steel pin or bodkin into the flesh. These bodkins could
be anything up to three inches long. The marks were thought to
be both insensitive to pain and unable to bleed as they had been
caused by the unnatural Devil. Some thought the lack of sensitivity
to be part of his attempts to hide the mark.

If a mark was not found on a suspected witch this was not
taken as evidence of innocence but that the witch had somehow
'hidden' the mark. This was also true where a mark 'disappeared'.
Suspected witches were often bodily searched by baillies or sheriffs
before the arrival of an official witch brodder. The baillie, having
found a mark, would record the same. When searched by the witch
brodder, if the mark was then found to be missing, this was taken
as proof not of any error by baillie or sheriff but as part of the
trickery of the witch in making the mark 'disappear'.

As the Devil's mark was so important, as one of the four proofs
of witchcraft, both Auld Nick and the witch would try their utmost
to hide the mark. The finding of the Devil's mark was, therefore,
the preserve of experts. These experts were licensed by the Privy
Council to brod witches when asked under a Commission. Unlike
local Commissioners, witch brodders were paid a fee in addition
to their expenses. Arriving in a small village by horse, and occasionally accompanied by a servant, the brodder needed food and
accommodation for himself and his servant and stabling for his
horse. All of which was paid for by the local community in addition to any fee charged. Depending on the length of time spent
on a case and the number of witches involved, the final fee could
be considerable. The involvement of a witch brodder constituted
a great financial cost to communities but even the smallest and
poorest villages accepted the burden content that a witch had been
found whatever the cost.

As in all aspects of human life where money is to be made, the
greedy, the venal and the plain charlatans are always to be found
and witch brodding was to be no exception. John Balfour plied his
trade as a brodder across Scotland in the early part of the century. In
1632, concerns were raised that he 'goes athort the countrie abusing
simple and ignorant people for his private gayne'.[44] He was called
before the Privy Council to answer these charges. The council were

not convinced as to his level of knowledge or expertise in the matter and he was forbidden from continuing to practise. Several questions remain unanswered. Why, prior to 1632, had he been able to work without any official warrant? Witch brodders could only work when a Commission to try a witch had been issued. Once this was set in motion, the local investigators, headed by the minister, would start their questioning. When a community had decided a brodder was needed, who had named Balfour, who had no official warrant from the Privy Council, as their man? Balfour does not appear to have acted as a brodder on a single occasion but on several; so who was employing him? Was his name known as someone who would find the Devil's mark with no questions asked? Interestingly, although barred from working as a brodder, no charges appear to have been laid against Balfour for the torture of accused witches brodded by him. All of the witches brodded by Balfour were executed.

In 1650, another brodder, George Caithie, fell under suspicion. Having spent several years previously working as a brodder and no doubt earning a goodly sum, Caithie's own greed was to be his downfall. This time it would be the Kirk who would catch him out. Jonet Coutts had been arrested and confessed to witchcraft before the Haddington presbytery in East Lothian. Jonet had, in her confession, named several other witches from East Lothian. Jonet, however, was from Peebles and did not know Haddington well; she had named several local women of good character. Jonet was brought before the interrogators to explain herself and confessed that she had struck a bargain with Caithie. The deal was a simple one. She was to name as many witches as possible. He would then be 'put to try anent the witches' mark and to profit thereby'[45] and would then try to get Jonet's sentence reduced from execution to a lesser penalty. Caithie was called before the Kirk to answer the charges. He gave a firm denial of any bargain charging Jonet as a lying witch. Unfortunately for Caithie, the Haddington Kirk did not believe him; the women named by Jonet had not just been of good character, they were known to the local minister as pious women that attended the Kirk regularly. The minister and the elders asked the civil authorities to deal with him. Although a request for arrest was made, no records remain as to whether or not this was carried out. Jonet was executed.

The use of witch brodding had another more sinister aspect. Authorised or not, the practice allowed those of a sadistic mind to ply their trade with the apparent blessing of the Kirk. One such appears to have been Jon Dick who, on more than one occasion, brodded suspected witches to death. Dick was arrested in 1662 and imprisoned in the tolbooth in Edinburgh. Complaints had been raised that he had worked without the required authority, had shaved and humiliated prisoners and that in some cases prisoners had been 'pricked to death'.[46]

There is no doubt that an inexperienced brodder might cause the accidental death of a prisoner by blood loss or shock. This does not appear to have been the situation in this case, however. Dick was accused of causing the death of more than one suspect. Privy Council records state that 'ane cheating fellow, named Jon Dick... thereafter pricking him [the suspected witch] to the great effusion of his blood and with much torture to his body'.[47] What is of the greatest concern to the Privy Council was the fact of him being 'ane cheating fellow'.[48] This challenge to their authority, by Dick overstepping the bounds in his treatment of prisoners, was their main concern. The Council noted the treatment and death of the suspected witches but seemed to accept this as a possible consequence of the work of a brodder. The disregard for the authority of the Council was another matter. Either Dick was working completely without a warrant from the Council or he was working and claiming to have such a warrant. In either case, he had shown a lack of respect for the authority and dignity of the Council. Although the Devil's mark was most commonly found on the head, shoulders and neck in Scotland, Dick would frequently have suspects stripped and shaved all over their bodies and would attempt to find the Devil's mark in their privy parts [genitalia]. This treatment of the suspects was superfluous to the charge of insulting the authority of the Privy Council and was not followed up with any known punishment. Within this mind-set, sadism could go on unchallenged.

The most famous witch brodder in Scotland was undoubtedly John Kincaid. A native of Tranent in East Lothian, he became famous throughout Scotland for his uncanny ability to find the Devil's mark on any witch no matter how cunningly hidden. Working between

1649 and 1662, it is not known how many witches were sent to the flames as a result of his work but the figure may well be in excess of 200.

In his time, Kincaid travelled between Edinburgh and the Lothians, as far north as Stirling and as far west as Glasgow, but he was most frequently to be found in the various towns of the Borders. Called in by the Kirk to help in the cases of uncooperative suspects, he travelled to towns and villages alike and would come as ready to brod 20 as one. His name is repeated time and time again in trial records right through the 1650s with the apparent blessing of the Privy Council. He, unlike brodders Balfour and Dick, was working with the requisite legal authority; at least initially.

In 1662, however, accusations were raised against Kincaid and a warrant was issued for his arrest by the Privy Council.[49] Two main charges were levelled at Kincaid: that he had wrongly found the Devil's mark on innocent victims and, more importantly, that he had been brodding suspects without having a warrant to do so. Kincaid, it seems, had succumbed like others to the witch hunting fever and had acted without due process of the law. The official report submitted to the Privy Council stated that Kincaid had worked 'without warrand and order to prick and try these persons'. More damning was the statement that 'there hath bein great abuses committed by John Kincaid', concluding that 'in all probabilitie many innocents have suffered'.[50] The numbers are not stated but records show several appeals by individuals pleading for release on the grounds that they had been unlawfully brodded and that other than the supposed Devil's mark found by Kincaid there was no evidence against them. The Privy Council had to act. Kincaid was arrested and sent to the tolbooth in Edinburgh.

It is not known when and why Kincaid started working without the necessary warrants that he had, presumably, previously always sought and obtained. Was it for personal reasons? Or was this under pressure from Kirk Ministers in far flung rural parishes anxious to consign a witch to the flames quickly and without waiting for the paperwork to be completed? Whatever the reason, it gave suspected witches a glimmer of hope and appeals against their treatment were lodged.

After some two months in gaol without any formal charges being laid against him, Kincaid petitioned the Privy Council for his release. This was granted after he had posted bail of £1,000 Scots and agreed that he would no longer work as a witch finder without the correct warrant. The Privy Council, although sufficiently alarmed by his behaviour to imprison him in the tolbooth in Edinburgh, seemed reluctant to formally charge him and bring him to trial. However, as he had been reported to have been working without a warrant, he could not just be released. The Council was also somewhat concerned that Kincaid, who was by now an old, infirm man, would die in gaol. The payment of bail and his agreement to seek the proper permissions for any future work satisfied the Council. They did not ban him from working as a witch brodder but merely accepted his assurance that he would always obtain a warrant to do so in the future. There is no record of any further action taken against Kincaid. The situation of the 'many innocents [that] have suffered' was quietly forgotten by the Privy Council. It is not recorded if any of those who appealed against Kincaid's treatment of them won their appeal but if they did not, a single record has survived. What is more probable is that Kincaid's release with no charges brought against him resulted in any appeals being set aside and the trials for witchcraft continuing as normal.

The £1,000 Scots Kincaid posted as surety was an extremely large sum of money which may in part answer why he had worked without warrants. To be able to raise £1,000 in a two-month period hints that he was, by this time in his life, a relatively wealthy man. It may well be that part, if not all, of that wealth had been generated by witch hunting. The temptation to work quickly and without warrant for money had proved a great temptation for other brodders. It may well be that Kincaid, too, fell victim to such a temptation.

Witch brodders were one of the few individuals involved in witchcraft trials that made a living. As they were paid for every witch they detected, it was in their own interests to find more witches. While some, no doubt, thought they were doing God's work, many others saw an opportunity to make money and a few to indulge in sadistic acts for their own pleasure. And for those who were carrying out God's work? At the hands of these men, and they were all men, some victims were brodded to death, while many more suffered extreme humiliation and pain. All of those who were brodded and found to have the Devil's mark were executed.

Although brodding fell into disuse in the latter half of the century as the many abuses came to light, it remained, for many in the Kirk as well as the Privy Council, the preferred method for uncovering the Devil's own. The problem was not felt to be with brodding but with those who professed to have the skill yet did not and, more importantly, with those who claimed the authority to work as witch brodders without any warrant from the Privy Council. Brodding was discouraged as the abuses called into question the authority of the Privy Council. With poor transport and communication links in the country, it became increasingly difficult for the Council to ensure that those who were working had the requisite permissions; especially as the number of witches and brodders increased. Equally, when fear struck a local community about witches, this could lead to the local authorities employing a witch brodding before applying for a Commission. This was most frequent where an accusation seemed weak. What if the accusation was merely part of a local panic? Finding the Devil's mark, even if by an unauthorised brodder, reinforced the initial charge and justified the time and expense of applying to the Privy Council for a Commission.

Had the Privy Council been able to develop a more robust system of authorisation and monitoring of witch brodders, the search for the Devil's mark with steel bodkins would, no doubt, have continued.

Yet again, however, what was officially discouraged continued in practice in many rural areas for some years to come. Unofficial, self-appointed witch hunters would, for a reasonable fee, help local parishes in the discovery of witches and in bringing them to confession through the discovery of their Devil's mark. Cases of brodding, which could be carried out over several weeks until a mark was found, were recorded as late as 1684 in the Borders.

8

Lauder, 1649

'the Devil is a lyar'

ACROSS THE MOOR from Stow, the guid folk of Lauder had watched and listened in horror at the events taking place in their small neighbour, ever thankful that the Lord had spared them. The involvement of the lad from Lauder in the Stow case was quickly dismissed as he was disowned by all in the town and the blame squarely laid at the door of adulterous Stow women who seduced young men. But as the year drew on, rumours grew that Lauder was not to be spared from the Devil and his ilk.

Hob (Robert) Grieve had lived in Lauder all his life and, although known throughout the town as a man who had married a witch, was thought no more than a harmless fool. His wife had been executed well over 20 years previously, a deserving shrew by local accounts, and Hob had managed to scrape a living by working here and there on odd jobs. One of the poorer inhabitants of the town, he was nonetheless a cheery fellow that liked nothing better that to sit with a pint of ale on a summer evening and talk of this and that. However, was the problem. Hob was a talker. He would talk at great length about what was happening in the town whether he knew the details or not. He would spin tales about great sights he had seen, although everyone knew he had never been further than the Gala Water. One evening sitting with some local worthies talking of the troubles in Stow Hob had let slip how his wife had taken him to meet a great gentleman at the Gala water just a little south of Stow. No more was said but a few glances were exchanged. Was this just another one of Hob's stories? Within the week, the minister came to call on Hob and after some close questioning Mr Byres saddled his horse and rode across the moor to speak to Mr Cleland, the minister at Stow.

Thomas Byres and John Cleland invited a third minister, John Veitch from Bassendean, to join them in their deliberations. John Veitch was known as a hard man who had refused to conform to episcopacy and in 1662 would be deprived of his parish. He was outlawed in 1680 and imprisoned in 1683. He returned to his parish in 1690 and, until his death in 1692, he stuck dogmatically to his belief in the inherent evil that was witchcraft and called for the sternest punishments possible to be meted out to those convicted of witchcraft.

The three ministers contemplated the case. Was Hob merely a gossiping fool, bragging when in his cups and with the Stow case so fresh in everyone's mind? Or was he a witch that had managed to escape justice by blaming his wife? After a night deep in thought, they made their decision and wrote to the Privy Council for a Commission to investigate and try Hob Grieve and any others he might delate as witches. John Veitch offered his services as an investigator into the case. William and Gilbert Lauder, the baillies, were instructed to bring Hob Grieve in for interrogation.

Hob was brought to the town's tolbooth to await a visit from the ministers. Armed with their Bibles, the three ministers had Hob brought before them. Asked if he knew why he had been brought before them, he answered simply 'forbye my wife was a witch'.[51] Prepared for a long and hard interrogation, the ministers were quite unprepared for what he said next. Hob told them that in 1629, he had been walking with his wife down at the Gala water near Stow. His wife, as always, was nagging him about his ways and said that she knew of a gentleman that would give him some good work and would help them get rich if they would but listen to him and do as they were bid. Hob then stated he saw a large mastiff dog, the like of which he had never seen before and which amazed him. Just as soon as he had seen the dog, it disappeared and a fine black man stood in his place. The gentlemen said if he, Hob, would become but an officer in his service, attend meetings on the Sabbath and hold the door for all to come in, he would be rich. Then Hob's tone changed and he sounded aggrieved as he told the ministers that Auld Nick had deceived him as he had remained poor all his days. When they came for his wife as a witch, it was true that the Devil had protected him but Hob had never become rich and had thus taken a 'richt scunnert wi him'.[52] But there was more to come. Hob then proceeded to tell the ministers of all the people he had seen at the meetings: Isobel Brotherstane, Margaret Dalgleish, Janet Lyes and Christian Smith. Hob stopped talking and grinned at the three shocked ministers. He was taken away to spend the night in the cells while Byres, Cleland and Veitch deliberated on what they had heard.

The next morning, Isobel Brotherstane came to the tolbooth and, calling Hob a warlock, demanded to speak to him. William Lauder told her to go home but she refused and repeated her demand to speak to Hob. Eventually he was brought out to see Isobel flanked by two baillie's men. Isobel challenged him, 'thou common thief, how dare thou for thy soul say that ever before this time thou saw me or I saw thee, or ever was in thy company, either alone or with others?'[53]

Hob turned to the baillie. 'How come she then to know that I called her a witch? Surely none but the Devil, thy old master and mine, has told thee so much?'[54]

Isobel replied, 'The Devil and thou perish together, for he is not my master though he be thine. I defy the Devil and all his works.'[55]

Hob then reminded her of all the times and places they had met while in Auld Nick's service.

Then Isobel replied again. 'Now I perceive that the Devil is a lyar and a murderer from the beginning, for this night he came to me, and told me to come and abuse thee; and never come away till I was confronted with thee, and he assured me that thou would deny all and say, thou false tongue, thou lyest.'[56]

Brought before the ministers, Isobel then confessed to witch-craft and delated the same names as Hob but then added another – Issobel Raich. This last name caused some concern to Thomas Byres. Issobel Raich was known as a god-fearing woman and he hesitated for a moment before taking down her name. When Margaret Dalgleish, Janet Lyes, and Christian Smith were brought in, they all confessed along with Isobel Brotherstane that, yes, they had denied their baptism and that they had gone into the service of the black gentleman but that he had deceived them and they were all still very poor. Other than Isobel Brotherstane, none of the others had named Issobel Raich as a fellow witch. Dalgleish, Lyes, Smith and Brotherstane were all in their 40s and widows with no close family. They were among the poorest of the women in Lauder being practically destitute with no prospects of any improvement in their lives. They may have attended meetings with Hob deluding themselves that the Devil had indeed promised them a better life or they may have confessed after the usual treatment in the tolbooth, the records do not exist to give any more detail.

Issobel Raich was slightly younger than the rest being in her early 30s. A married woman with children and a working husband, she was not poor by the standards of the day. Able to afford to have food and clothing brought into the tolbooth, she also did not suffer as much as her fellow prisoners. It does appear, however, that her husband abandoned her soon after her imprisonment. Who, therefore, was arranging the delivery of the food and clothing she received?

The trial date was set for 2 October and Thomas Cranston, Edzer Young of Wedderlie, Robert Hart of St John's chapel and Alexander Hume sat as Magistrates. The six accused sat in Lauder tolbooth to wait for the trial. It was assumed that Hob had been their leader and as such was kept apart from the others. Stories started to circulate about his powers and the baillie and his men spent as little time as possible with their fearsome prisoner. Left to himself, confined to a cramped airless cell over the hot summer months, Hob lost what little wits he had originally had and slowly went mad. He was heard shouting and laughing in his cell which merely added to his reputation.

The trial was initially a subdued affair. Margaret Dalgleish, Janet Lyes, Christian Smith and Isobel Brotherstane were brought into the court room and sat as the charges against them and their confessions were read out and duly recorded. A few background details as to their character were also stated. The atmosphere changed with the arrival of Hob. Brought into court, he was a dreadful sight. He had lost weight during his time in the tolbooth and his clothes, which were very ragged, lay loose on his frame. His hair was long and unkempt, matched by his beard and he gave off a powerful and foul smell. Muttering to himself under his breath, curses and spells some said, he appeared to disregard the magistrates when questioned. John Veitch stepped up and read out his previous confession as a servant of the Devil. Hob laughed and said that he didn't care much for him anymore. He said that the Devil had once tried to drown him at Musselburgh when he had been carrying a heavy creel upon his back. Hob then said that he had a secret to tell but would tell only Mr Veitch. Shuffling up to the minister, Hob said that Auld Nick had come to him several times while he lay in the prison and told him he would cast him into the fire. Hob told the Minister that he didn't care and wasn't sacred as he was more powerful than the Devil now and could defeat him any time he chose.

It took the jury only one day to find Hob Grieve, Isobel Brotherstane, Margaret Dalgleish, Janet Lyes and Christian Smith guilty of witchcraft. The magistrates sentenced them to be worriet and then burnt. Mad Hob might have been but he was still to face the flames.

Issobel Raich had sat quietly and had drawn herself a little apart from the others during the trial and when her confession was read out, there was debate as to whether or not it was indeed a true confession or perhaps a story uttered by the fears of a frivolous woman. Mention was also made of her previous good character – this was no quarrelsome dame – but these were severely brushed aside by John Veitch. Unfortunately for Issobel, she had been delated by a confessed witch and so her guilt was obvious. She too was sentenced to death.

On the day of her execution, Issobel Raich spoke to the crowd. 'Now all you that see me this day, know that I am to die a witch by my own confession; and I free all men, especially the Ministers and Magistrate, of the guilt of my blood. I take it wholly on myself. My blood be upon my own head; and as I must make answer to the God of heaven presently, I declare I am as free of witchcraft as any child; but being delated by a malicious woman, and put in prison under the name of a witch, disowned by my husband and friends, and seeing no ground of hope of my coming out of prison or ever coming in credit again, through a temptation of the Devil, I made up that confession on purpose to destroy my own life, being weary of it, and choosing rather to die than to live.'[57]

It was said that the 'temptation of the Devil' had been an affair that Isobel was rumoured to have had with a member of the local nobility; and the real reason for her abandonment by her husband. Alexander Hume, one of the presiding magistrates, had tried to have her confession disallowed and had sought her release. This had been vehemently blocked by John Veitch. After her execution, it was strongly rumoured that a servant of Alexander Hume had been seen visiting the tolbooth carrying fresh food and clean clothing.

Hob Grieve, Joke the Graham; there are few men named in the Scottish witchcraft trial records but they are there. The most infamous was Dr Fian, leader of the North Berwick witches who had tried to drown the King. Scotland, however, like most European countries saw witchcraft in terms of a female crime. In contrast, most Scandinavian countries disputed the usefulness of women to the Devil. Why, they argued, if the Devil was really trying to attack the Godly would he use stupid women? In the Scandinavian witch trial records, the numbers of men accused is well over 60 per cent. In Scotland, it was the weak, lustful and easily corrupted women that became Auld Nick's wanton followers. But what about the men in Scotland? What was their role and how did they fare in the courts? Around 16 per cent of those tried in Scotland as witches were men; the figure in the Borders was lower – around 8 per cent or some 28 of those in the existing records. Of those, most were listed as warlocks, not witches. The difference between the two was subtle but important. A witch was, in essence, a handmaiden of the Devil, a follower who would do his bidding. A warlock was considered more of a disciple of Auld Nick.

Warlocks troubled the Kirk for three main reasons. Firstly, men, by their very nature, were considered steadfast and true in their faith, as opposed to women, and unlikely therefore to make a pact with the Devil. And if part of that pact, as was fervently believed by the Kirk, had involved intercourse with the Devil taking advantage of the lustful nature of women, where did that leave warlocks? Not even the most zealous of Kirk elders suggested homosexual relations. The taking of an oath with the Devil could, however, entail the warlock kissing him on his arse. Another notion dreamt up by the men of the Kirk. No such claim was made by a female witch. While homosexuality was not unknown in 17th century Scotland – James VI had had several male lovers – it was a crime punishable by death and was anathema to the Kirk. The problem for the clergy was how to expose and condemn such practices without drawing them to the attention of young men who might be curious. The Kirk was terrified that even the mention of such acts would pollute the young. Of course, some Kirk members would have been homosexual, even if they did not admit it to themselves. This situation becomes even more ludicrous when it is known that homosexuality was, if not approved of, then at least accepted and in most cases tolerated as a matter of fact by many ordinary people. Reivers such as 'buggerback Elliot' and 'bangtail Armstrong' had been well known in the Borders in the 16th century.

The second issue with warlocks concerned authority. Most crimes in witchcraft trials involved the laying on of sickness or ruining crops and ale – the concerns of women, not the crimes of men. This was probably why most men accused were classed as warlocks rather than witches. Where warlocks were involved. it was in leadership roles over several female witches. The crimes of which a warlock was accused might be of a lowly nature but the natural order of male dominance over female was restored by the directions for such crimes being given by a warlock while the work was carried out by witches. However, as warlocks could hold leadership over women, did this mean that they acted as an intermediary between the Devil and the witches? This was a further terrifying development. Did warlocks intercede between Auld Nick and witches in the way Catholic priests had between God and the people? For the Protestant clergy, this reinforced ideas as to the diabolical nature of the Catholic priesthood but also raised the possibility that the Devil was creating his own church on Earth. This was theologically worrying territory.

The last troubling element for the Kirk was the actual nature of a warlock. A comforting thought might have been that every warlock was addled in his wits. But while Hob Grieve may well have become mad as his treatment and incarceration had continued, there are no records to suggest that only the feeble minded were arrested and charged with being a warlock. The problem for the Kirk was in the very name, warlock. A witch was a woman who had denied God and given herself to the Devil; a warlock was an oath-breaker. The Kirk demanded that men take responsibility for their belief: they were expected to pledge a solemn oath and covenant with God. A warlock, by taking up with Auld Nick, had made a conscious decision to break that oath. Time and again, the Bible exhorted the faithful to keep their oath to God. To become a warlock was to break that oath. In the eyes of the Kirk, there was no greater crime a man could commit.

There were of course certain men who, in the eyes of many, were already warlocks in all but name: Catholics. The heresy of the Catholic faith was anathema to the Kirk, a grey area for the courts and a political minefield for all. As Catholics, they were denying the true faith but were, frustratingly, not under its juris-diction. The Reformation had been successful in Scotland and the country was indeed a Protestant one but in pockets here and there the Catholics remained. Although very much in the minority in the Borders, memories were long and Francis Stewart, Earl of Bothwell's involvement in the witchcraft case of North Berwick had not been forgotten. Acquitted of all charges against him, no doubt by diabolical means, he had later revealed his true nature by rejecting the true faith and becoming a Catholic. As an illegitimate son of James V and a member of the nobility, he was a terrifying example to the Kirk of the heights to which diabolical Catholics could reach.

There was also one type of warlock feared above all others and that was the minister or elder who was also a warlock. Diabolical Catholics may have evoked hatred in the Kirk but members of the Kirk themselves who broke their oath to God was surely a sign of the apocalypse. The most famous was Major Thomas Weir. Born in Carluke in 1599, Weir was the son of the Laird of Kirkton. He was a signatory to the Solemn League and Covenant and served in the Covenanter army. In 1650, he became commander of the Edinburgh Town Guard. While commander, he began each day by leading the town guard in prayer. A powerful orator, his fame quickly spread and locals soon started to come to his house at the top of the West Bow in Edinburgh to hear these morning prayers. Before long, Weir was preaching every morning and he was given the title of the Bowhead Saint by the crowds who came to hear him. He was the epitome of God's Elect and Kirk elders across Scotland held him up as an example of such. Young ministers would travel to Edinburgh just to hear him preach.

In 1670, Weir fell ill and, as he would later claim, when in the grip of a wild fever confessed to several crimes. He was arrested along with his spinster sister Jean, known as Grizel, who had been his housekeeper. The pair were taken to the Edinburgh tolbooth. Under questioning, Grizel confirmed Weir's confession admitting to several acts of witchcraft and sorcery. According to Grizel, her brother had been taken to Dalkeith by a stranger in a 'fiery' coach and had 'supernatural intelligence' of the defeat of the Scot's army at Worcester the day it happened (3 September 1651). Weir's power, according to Grizel, came from his walking stick which he had been given secretly by the stranger. The walking stick was endowed with special powers contained in the carved human head that sat atop the shaft, the same carved head that Weir would stroke when deep in thought. Although Grizel appeared addled in her wits, the authorities confronted Weir with her confession whereupon he not only confirmed most of what she had said but then added more detail of his own as to the crimes he had committed aided by evil powers. Most of the crimes involved causing illness on other members of God's Elect. He also informed his interrogators that he and his sister had been having an incestuous relationship since he had taken up his post as city commander and begun his preaching. He was not, however, ashamed in any way about the relationship.

The Weirs were both found guilty of witchcraft and consorting with the Devil and sentenced to death. The crimes committed by one so outwardly pious, a member of the Kirk and one who had been known as saint (another name for one of God's Elect) had shocked all in the Kirk. Weir was sentenced to be worriet and burned and the minister presiding over his execution urged him at the end to pray for forgiveness. Weir replied, saying, 'Let me alone, I will not, I have lived as a beast, and I must die as a beast.'[58] The court had ordered that Weir's walking stick was also to be burnt. Several onlookers noted that it made 'rare turnings'[59] in the flames as it burned and the mouth of the carved head appeared to gape open, as if attempting to utter some final diabolical words.

Thomas Weir was a rarity but the crimes he had allegedly committed for so long and in a position of power in the capital all the while preaching the word of God made him a byword of evil. That a man of God could be ensnared by the Devil like a foolish and weak woman was a reality that horrified and troubled the Kirk. In the case of less notorious warlocks, the more wicked the crimes committed, the less troubled although more horrified, the Kirk became as this followed the natural order of things. As men were the superior of women so warlock, as men, should have been engaged in crimes more worthy of the male sex. Raising bad weather was typical of this, either to ground ships off the Berwickshire coast or to close the drove roads across the moors. Witches might be single women at the bottom of the pile as far as earnings and respect went but most warlocks were men of middling status, not individuals at the edges of communities. Many were farmers, small merchants and artisans with a certain standing in rural towns and villages. Their crimes were often aimed at those with similar businesses. The failure of a fellow trader would be to their advantage or revenge could be sought where a previous business transaction had resulted in a loss of money or respect. These then were crimes that the Kirk, although condemning, could understand.

As men, suspected warlocks were not passive female defendants; although plenty women proved to be pretty formidable. These were men that would resist arrest, demand a legal defence, cross-examine witnesses and turn cases on their heads as they voiced counter-accusations and argument. A witch delated by a warlock would face the flames every time. A warlock accused by a witch could, by sheer force of personality and using the accepted norms of the day, not only walk free but lay charges against the women that had delated him and also the local sheriff and minister for false arrest and imprisonment. These were not men to be trifled with, whereas the very nature of women laid them open to charges of witchcraft while their status in society weighed against them in the courts. For men, the very opposite was true. Seldom suspected, when delated, it was often dismissed as the spite and deceit of women. In some cases, witches who delated a man of good standing had the accusation of malice added to the list of their own diabolical crimes.

Even when arrested, many warlocks were given bail and allowed to wait their time until trial at home. The courts, filled with male lawyers, prosecutors and juries, did not want to believe fellow men guilty and when the accused put up a robust defence, not guilty and not proven verdicts were frequently returned. Those who were found guilty were often old or poor or had lost their wits and even then could sometimes escape the flames merely to be flogged and excommunicated.

The majority of warlocks tried in the Borders were related to witches and as relatives would naturally have come under suspicion. The familiar tale of mundane sickness in children and kye was told and the Kirk interrogated and prosecuted. The theological drama of oath breaking sat side by side with accusations of charms and spells. While the records show a lower rate of both conviction and execution for warlocks than for witches, there is a higher rate of suicide. Was the loss of status and respect too great for these men to bear? Was the accusation of being thought an oath-breaker too shameful to face? Even though the conviction rate was lower for men than for women, it was still higher in witchcraft cases than in most other crimes. Conviction and execution as a warlock meant an individual's estate was forfeit to the crown. For men with families, this could result in their wives and children being left destitute. Families would lose their savings, business and homes, in addition to being shunned by their communities. Although death by suicide was a sin and would debar the corpse from burial in consecrated ground, it at least allowed the family to inherit from the dead man's estate. Widows were allowed to continue in business and thus provide for their family. In some cases, the widows of suicides were even given financial aid by the Kirk.

Male accused also tended to have greater access than women to the means by which to end their lives. As men with a degree of status denied most women, the accused could argue against his accusation at the earliest stage and at the very least demand to be spared the ordeal of gaol, although this was not always the case for destitute men. Bound over in their own homes until the trial, male suspects had the means and opportunity to kill themselves. For those that were incarcerated, money would, no doubt, buy a stout rope and an hour of time when the guard would be conveniently elsewhere. As poorer members of the community, such opportunities were denied their female counterparts. Of the recorded suicides in the Borders, 67 per cent were male, 22 per cent were female with the remaining 11 per cent of unknown gender. There are no records in the Borders for any male suicide by those accused of a crime that was not witchcraft.

9

Kelso, 1662

'pilliewinkles upon her fingers...

a grevious torture'

THE SPRING OF 1662 was a mild one. The last famine had been over 14 years previously and while not exactly a distant memory, neither was it a constant spectre to the villagers of Kelso. Lying on the banks of the Tweed where it joins with the Teviot, Kelso was, in 1662, a remarkably quiet village. Barely ten miles from the border with England, it had seen armies come and go in the past and would do so again but as the spring turned to summer it was no enemy army that would trouble the village but a woman, two children, an old woman and a Covenanter.

On 12 June, Sir Archibald Douglas obtained a Commission from the Privy Council to try four accused: Bessie Thomson, Malie Jonstoun, Agnes Quarie and Malie Turnbull, on the grounds that they had all confessed to being witches. The Commission stated that Sir Douglas was to judge the four women and if found guilty without the application of torture or other indirect means to extract confession 'then and in these cases the said commissioners (to) cause the sentence of death to be execute upon them and no otherways'.[60] The Commission was similar to hundreds of others that had been sought and issued throughout the century to various towns in the Borders with two crucial differences.

This Commission appeared, on the face of it, to prohibit the Commissioners from using torture or other indirect means to extract confession. Torture was routinely used and an acceptable practice until around 1661 and even thereafter its use was allowed as long as the correct permissions were sought. Indirect means such as sleep deprivation and walking were not considered torture but again were an accepted method by which to bring witches to confession and for which no permission was required. Why therefore, should the Privy Council wish to stop the use of torture and especially indirect means in this case and why should they specify this within the Commission document itself? Was this merely the prescribed wording about torture that had been agreed should be placed in every Commission granted by the Privy Council after 1661, or was something else going on?

The second difference was found in a later paragraph where the Commission states that the accused had to be both mentally and legally competent before any confession could be accepted. While those considered mentally incompetent had been known to stand trial, as had children, again the question arises. Why should the Privy Council have specified in this case that those standing trial had to be sane and above the legal age of responsibility? Local Commissioners knew the law, there was no need to state the bar on children or mental competency. Why was the Privy Council so concerned about legal procedures in Kelso?

Sir Archibald Douglas was a fervent Covenanter and was extremely outspoken in his condemnation of, as he saw it, any form of religious belief that was not strictly Presbyterian. Unfortunately, for any accused witches brought before him, this meant that interrogations carried out under Sir Archibald's jurisdiction were extreme in nature and all-encompassing in their application. Being addled in your wits or under the age of 16 was no protection from Sir Archibald's questioning. While the questioning of such individuals was allowed in witchcraft cases, it was to be done with care and any testimony that arose was to be treated with caution. Given Sir Archibald's personality and beliefs, it is unlikely much care would be taken. Moreover, the Commission was to try four accused, not witnesses. As the Privy Council had raised the issue of age, it may be either that some of the four accused were below the age of 16, or that Sir Archibald had on previous occasions put children to torture.

Bessie Thomson, Malie Jonstoun, Agnes Quarie and Malie Turnbull had all apparently confessed to some degree of witchcraft, although the exact details are not known. Arrested by Sir Archibald, they were imprisoned and immediately interrogated. Whatever wickedness they confessed, it was enough for Sir Archibald and he applied to the Privy Council for a Commission. Initially, the Privy Council asked for more details before a Commission would be granted. This in itself was unusual. Most Commissions were granted with few, if any, stipulations. The Privy Council was overwhelmed by applications and did not create any more work for itself than necessary. It was also at that early stage in the proceedings that the Privy Council imposed the stipulations about torture, age and mental competency. The more detailed confessions, as demanded by the Privy Council, were to be obtained without torture and legal age and competence were to be ascertained and certified. The inference appears to be that Bessie, Malie, Agnes and Malie's first partial confessions to Sir Archibald had been obtained under torture. There is, also some evidence to suggest that at least some of the accused were either children or mentally incompetent.

The Privy Council stated that they wished to see recorded the details of how the accused had renounced their baptism and had made a pact with the Devil. The Council wanted details of the pact. How had it been made? What had been said? What had been signed? Who had been there? Where had it taken place and when? The Kirk was exacting in its interrogation in these matters. This was, after all, the dark heart of the whole matter. However, these were details that only a competent adult could provide. The Privy Council, it seemed, knew Sir Archibald only too well. Without recourse to torture and with only children and those mentally impaired to question, the case fell. This is not to suppose the Privy Council of being concerned about the four accused no matter how young or senile. Rather, they wished correct legal process to be followed and possibly, at the same time, to temper Sir Archibald and his local power.

While the Privy Council were attempting to curb the covenanting excesses of Sir Archibald, from the safety of their Edinburgh chambers of course, the reality for the accused witches was somewhat different. The ages of the accused are not recorded but both Bessie Thomson and Malie Jonstoun would be in trouble with the authorities some 20 years later when they were described as being women in their late 20s or early 30s. This would seem to suggest that in 1662, when they were tortured by Sir Archibald, they could have been as young as eight or nine. Agnes Quarie would also be questioned in later years when she would be dismissed as an old woman too fond of 'seeing the faeries'.[61] And this was not a new development, apparently Agnes had been 'odd' all her life.

While all four accused were not executed, they had suffered illegal imprisonment, interrogation and torture. They would have suffered, at the very least, sleep deprivation, psychological bullying and having been walked for hours on end. They might have been burnt with hot stones, had their skin rasped off with ropes or their fingers broken and crushed. They may well have been beaten by their guards, partly for fun or boredom, or from a genuine hatred of witches. All of this as well as being imprisoned for weeks away from their families and friends. They would have eaten little or poor-quality food, slept on filthy flea-infested straw with only a corner of their cell to relieve themselves. Even on release, they bore the stigma of having been investigated for witchcraft. The later trials of Bessie Thomson and Malie Jonstoun both make note of their previous interrogation by Sir Archibald being described in the court records as 'well known witches', the dreaded bad reputation seen as proof of being a witch. Sir Archibald may have been thwarted in his zeal in pursuing this particular case but no records exist of any charges brought against him for his initial and illegal ill treatment of Bessie, Malie, Agnes and Malie. In addition, this challenge from the authorities did little to dampen his fervour as his name appears as a prosecuting Commissioner in several cases over the following ten years.

While the existence of witches was, to the Kirk, self-evident, proof had to be brought before the Courts. The Witchcraft Act of 1563 stated that:

> forsamekeill as the Quenis Maiestie and thre Estatis in this present Parliament being informit that the havy, abominabill superstitioun usit be divers of the liegis of this Realme be using of Witchcraftis, Sorsarie, and Necromancie, and credence gevin thairto in tymes bygane aganis the Law of God: and for avoyding and away putting of all sic vane superstitioun in tymes tocum; It is statute and ordanit be the Quenis Maiestie and thre Estatis forsaidis that na maner of persoun nor persounis of quhatsumever estate, degre, or conditioun thay be of tak upone hand in ony tymes heirefter to use ony maner

of Wichcraftis, Sorsarie, or Necromancie: nor gif thame selfis furth to have ony sic craft or knawlege thairof, thairthrow abusand the pepill; Nor that na persoun seik ony help, response, or consultatioun at ony sic usaris(or abusaris) forisaidis of Wichcraftis, Sorsarie, and Necromancie, under the pane of: dead asweill to be execute aganis the user-abusar, as the seiker of the response or consultatioun.And this to be put to execution be the Justice Schireffis, Stewartis, Baillies, Lordis of Regaliteis and Rialteis, thair Deputis, and uthers Ordinar Jugeis competent within this Realme with all rigour, having powar to execute the samin.[62]

The Act was therefore clear: the interrogation of witches was to be executed 'with all vigour'. Witches had to be made to confess by whatever means necessary. If proof was needed then interrogation would produce that proof. They had to be made to name any other witches involved and also what they had done in their dealings with Auld Nick and in their evil acts. And of course the Devil's mark had to be found on their body. But they were witches and had magical powers – why did they not escape from prison and from their treatment? They had in fact been abandoned. The Devil, who had promised them everything, was a liar and deceiver and this was proved by the fact that he had abandoned them to their fate. He has deserted them to face the torments of their treatment alone. And once made to realise they had been abandoned, the witches would confess. This was the reasoning that lay behind the torture of witches.

Torture was freely allowed up to 1661 and if it was to be used thereafter, permission had to be sought. And it was rarely refused. However, permission often entailed sending a rider with a dispatch off to Edinburgh and awaiting a reply, which could take several days to appear and cost money. As witch hunts and the attendant hysteria mounted, local courts carried out interrogations with whatever methods they felt necessary, often dispensing with their duty to seek the permission of the Privy Council. Speed was of the essence in the fight against the Devil and his hordes and zealous Kirk elders applied torture, safe in the knowledge of their own righteousness and confident in the guilt of the accused even if the necessary permission had not been sought or had not yet arrived. In cases where permission had been given, local justice could often go far beyond what was legally allowed. This was a battle for the very souls of men and a little extra rough treatment here and there was preferable to allowing Auld Nick and his followers to overrun the earth. Records indicate that torture, whether legally sanctioned or not, was commonly used in the Borders as late as 1690.

There were several types of torture, each of which were developed to cause the maximum amount of pain in as quick a time as possible. In addition to the pain caused by the torture, most had long term effects well known to the victim which gave an added psychological stress to the physical pain endured.

One of the most common forms of torture was the pilliewinkles. These were long metal boards that fitted snugly over the fingers and had additional bands that wound round the fingers. The bands could be screwed tight by means of a pin. As the pilliewinkles were screwed tight, the fingers were crushed and the bones broken. In addition, the fingernails were frequently dragged out by the roots when the pilliewinkles were removed. The applications of the pilliewinkles, if carried out correctly, were often so painful that some victims fell unconscious and some were even said to die from shock. The pilliewinkles were particularly feared – and for good reason. For those found not guilty of witchcraft or not sentenced to death, the application of the pilliewinkles would, nevertheless, render the suspect crippled for life. Unable to work in a rural economy like the Borders, the individual was instantly rendered destitute, reduced to begging. With a reputation tainted by witchcraft, Christian charity might well prove wanting and death by starvation was the most likely outcome.

Ropes were also commonly used as a torture method. A length of rope would be wound round the victim's forehead and then twisted tight to apply pressure. This would twist and burn the skin and hair would often be wrenched out by the roots. Blood vessels, especially those in the eyes and nose, would rupture and bleed profusely. Depending on the severity and length of treatment, the victim could be left blind, as the eyes were damaged by knots in the ropes, and deaf as the ear drums could be perforated. An account from the Newes from Scotland of 1591 lists the treatment of one witch: 'the pilliewinkles upon her fingers, which is a grevious torture, and binding and wrenching her head with a cord or rope, which is a most cruel torture... and then she confessed all.'[63] Left blind and deaf by this torture, the victim was once again reduced to a destitute beggar.

Suspects could also be burnt with hot stones. The local black-smith would be called in to help in this matter, his expertise with fire integral to the procedure. The stones were heated in a pit and then spread in front of the victim who, barefoot, was made to stand on top of them. Victims who struggled too much or were unable to stand due to fatigue or previous ill treatment had the stones held against the soles of their feet. Although found to be an effective torture, as the feet can be very sensitive, this was infrequently used due to the cost of the blacksmith's time. While extremely painful at the time of application, the individual could potentially recover from such torture in time. This was provided, of course, that the wounds on the feet did not become infected in the filthy conditions in which the accused was held, in which case gangrene could set in and the toes or entire foot might require to be amputated.

The boot was another favoured method of extracting infor-mation. This comprised a large wooden boot that had holes in it through which further wooden pegs could be driven. The pegs could tear muscles, tendon and ligaments, and break bones in the foot and lower leg. The excruciating pain was not the only con-sideration. Like the pilliewinkles, the boot could render a victim a cripple for the rest of their life, unable to earn a livelihood and under threat of starvation.

Hairshirts or hairshifts were also used. Made out of very coarse material similar to sacking, they could, in some instances, shear a victim's skin off. More generally, the skin would become raw with bleeding and extremely painful. The accused witch was forced to wear this for days on end. Most then developed skin infections from the dirt and excrement that were also around in the cells. These infections, combined with the poor diet and gen-eral ill treatment endured while under arrest, contributed to the many deaths in gaol – especially of those with underlying illnesses or disease due to poverty or old age. Even when not forced to wear a hairshirt, suspects often had no other clothing with which to cover themselves in winter.

Sleep deprivation and walking were also carried out. These were not classed as torture and so could be applied at will. Sleep deprivation was a very effective way of obtaining confessions because it quickly led to hallucination and broke the individual's will, making them compliant with their interrogators. Desperate for sleep and with little understanding of what was actually happening, suspects readily responded to whatever question was put to them simply in order to be allowed to rest. It was usually undertaken by local authorities such as burgh baillies, or more frequently by the Kirk elders. Quite simply, accused witches were kept sitting on small stools and not allowed to put their feet on the ground for hours on end or told to stand up in a cell and not allowed to sit or lie down sometimes for two or more days.

Walking was equally brutal and was again carried out under the supervision of the Kirk elders. Two strong young men would take the suspected witch under each arm and walk her up and down her cell for around two hours. The two men would then be relieved by two fresh walkers. This could be continued for anything up to 48 hours at a stretch. By the end of this time, the prisoner would be exhausted; their feet and lower legs would be a pulpy and bloody mess. The blood loss and shock could result in death from dehydration and hypovolaemic shock. If the individual did not die, and the balllies knew exactly when to stop, they would probably be suffering from neuralgic pain in their legs which would be exacerbated afterwards by the lightest touch so that the baillies only had to tap the leg for it to send excruciating pain up to the small of the back. This treatment could also prove long-lasting with individuals left yet again unfit for rural work.

Swimming witches was seldom used in Scotland, although it was used in a case in 1597. The records are scarce for that time but it appears to have been discredited in some way and was not used thereafter. This method was devised as a test to see whether or not the suspect floated, the belief being that the water would reject them as they had obviously rejected the baptism of Christ. The suspect was tied with ropes in such a way as to allow them to float but also to prevent them drowning. It was, however, a test that was open to abuse with many being drowned as a result of poor technique or perhaps deliberate malice. Female clothing with wide apron pockets was particularly easy to tie in such a manner as to create air pockets which allowed the accused to float. This may have been the reason why it was not used in Scotland after 1597. The practice of swimming witches was common in England as it was for the accused in several other crimes.

Several court records list the methods used to extract confessions:

> bound her armes with towes and so threw the same about that they disjoynted and mutilat both her armes.[64]

> tying their thumbs behind them and then hanging them up by them... set lighted candles to their feet and between their toes and in their mouths and burned their heads.[65]

> the women were tortured by hanging them up by the thombes and burning the soles of their feet at the fyre.[66]

During all of these practices the suspects would be being constantly berated by the local Kirk minister and elders. Harangued and bullied, they would be told that they were evil and wicked and would go straight to hell for all eternity for their crimes; told how they were a disgrace and a source of shame and loathing to their families; how everybody hated and feared them, their filthy practices were known, their heresies had been exposed. Castigated as the Devil's whores and followers, they were ridiculed and humiliated. This psychological abuse was heaped on them continuously in a tirade of anger and disgust. Those who refused to co-operate could also be threatened that their families would be arrested and also tortured. This was often used where a suspect had a teenage daughter or son.

Their treatment in gaol was also harsh. While prison conditions were hard for all prisoners at that time, they were particularly brutal for suspected witches. All prisoners had to pay for their own food and bedding and would sell anything they had to prevent starvation. However, many had nothing to sell. Most ordinary prisoners had basic food and bedding supplied by the local Kirk. This largesse was not, however, extended to suspected witches. This left the accused dependent on friends and relatives. However, the stigma of a charge of witchcraft was often enough to drive away any that could help. Some no doubt feared the association with a witch and possible involvement in any further charges that were laid; some were scared of the accused witch herself. Visits from friends and family who brave enough to want to visit were frequently denied in case they brought the accused witch any aid. With little help forthcoming for the individual in gaol, the accused had to survive on basic water and gruel, with little clothing and bedding and no sanitation all the while being subjected to torture.

Cases of witchcraft could take several weeks to investigate before coming to trial and, although many trials lasted only a matter of days, some could last several more weeks so that victims were often close to starving by the end of their ordeal. In addition, sanitation was as good as non-existent and several weeks' build-up of urine and excrement would render the air in the gaol foul and increase the likelihood of illness and disease and infection of any open wounds.

While the Kirk was involved in witch cases at every level and supervised torture sessions, they did not take any responsibility for the welfare of the suspects. The plight of suspected witches was noted with cases recorded where the accused were reduced to 'drinking their own piss.'[67] There are several instances of magistrates complaining about half-naked prisoners appearing before them in rags, the complaint being that their stench offended the noses of the authorities, not that they had been starved. Within the Borders, at least 15 individuals died of ill-treatment in gaol before being brought to trial. As their bodies were frequently buried quietly away from prying eyes in unmarked graves, rumours started of accused witches who had escaped justice and had been 'rescued' by the Devil. The authorities took a dim view of this and would frequently reprimand gaolers who had allowed accused witches to die. Little was done, however, to mitigate the conditions in which the accused were held. As far as the Kirk was concerned, the 15 individuals who died before trial and, therefore, before a guilty verdict had been passed were still deemed to have been guilty. Gaolers were reprimanded not so much that their treatment had been overly harsh but that they had not keep a better watch on the accused to prevent such convenient tricks as death with which the witches had escaped justice.

Alongside 'official' torture, there were also many cases where suspects were simply beaten until they confessed. While there are very few records of complaints against beatings by Kirk ministers, they do exist. What has been recorded, however, in the costings of one interrogation, is the bill for two stout Kirk men to 'compel said prisoner' and, on one occasion, for a new staff for the minister which had been broken in one beating. Such beatings were illegal but usually accepted as necessary and the suspect's own fault for showing such intransigence in refusing to confess. Any sympathy shown was for those ministers who had to deal with such foul creatures.

It is true that the treatment of any prisoner in the 17th century was far from perfect and ill treatment and torture could and frequently was used in many instances. However, witchcraft appears to be the only crime where ill treatment was ordered, supervised and in some instances carried out by Kirk ministers. The records also seem to indicate that, far from being used as a means of last resort, as in most other crimes, torture of one kind or another was automatically used from the moment of arrest in the case of witchcraft. It is also the only crime in which age, gender and infirmity did not appear to stay the hand or lessen the ill treatment.

10

Gallowshiels, 1668

'her petticoats a' agape'

GALLOWSHIELS IN THE 1600s was known as a small town north of its more important and prosperous neighbour Selkirk. Created as a burgh in 1599, by the mid-17th century its population had started to rise, attracted mainly by the work available in the town's three mills. With a population around 700, it had the usual mix of rich and poor with most of the latter crowded into the centre. The town, in common with so many in the Borders, saw several witch trials over the century. In most of the trials, the familiar pattern would be seen of the poor and the dispossessed being brought before the courts. In the case of Gallowshiels, the dominant families were the Pringles and the Scotts and members from both families sat as Commissioners. As the century wore on, the sons of previous Commissioners would take the place of their fathers sitting in judgement in the witchcraft trials. 1668 was no exception. A Commission was granted against Jonet Armstrong with James Pringle of Buckholme, George Pringle of Torwoodlee, James Pringle of Torwoodlee, Sir James Pringle of Gallowshiels, William Scott of Gallowshiels and Sir William Scott of Harden acting as Commissioners.[68] Each was either the son of a previous Commissioner or was the father of a future Commissioner.

Jonet had previously been known in and around Gallowshiels as a healer and midwife for over 30 years. By the time of her arrest in 1668, however, she was an old woman crippled with arthritis and going blind. Her age was not recorded for certain but she was said to be at least as old as the century itself. Always poor, she was now almost destitute and eked out her life by begging for alms from neighbours, relying on the memory of past service to families in times of illness and crisis. The giving of alms was expected from those who could afford it, as a Christian duty, and in cases like Jonet's could make the difference between life and death.

Jonet had lived in Gallowshiels all her life and was described as an indweller of the town.[69] Although an old woman, she does not appear to have had a bad reputation as there is no note of her in previous records. The local Kirk session records also hold no mention of her in their long list of admonishments for parishioners who failed to attend on a Sunday or whose behaviour was found wanting in some other manner. Jonet, presumably, knew who to approach for alms and who to avoid and the townsfolk probably looked on her, if not kindly, at least as nothing more than a harmless nuisance. However, in the spring of 1668, for some reason that is not recorded, that attitude changed and Jonet suddenly became a dame of ill repute. She had angered a neighbour in some way; perhaps she had asked for some bread and milk just one time too many, perhaps she had been refused and had walked away muttering. Whatever the cause, the neighbour complained to the local minister who summoned Jonet to appear before him and the Kirk elders.

There appears to have been some delay in Jonet appearing before the elders and, in that time, the list of offences had already started to increase. She was not always present in the Kirk of a Sunday, despite the lack of her name being noted in the Kirk sessions records. She was said to have muttered curses under her breath at several of her neighbours and – the inevitable charge – she was thought to have lain an illness on someone's child a few years previously.

By the time she was brought before the Kirk elders, their minds may well have been set. Unfortunately for Jonet, she was to provide further proof of her wickedness by her very appearance. She was ushered into the presence of the minister and the elders dressed in the only clothes she possessed. A destitute old woman in a dirty, tattered dress, the minister was outraged to note that she stood before them with 'her petticoats a' agape'.[70] This affront to the dignity of the Kirk was added to the list of offences against her and armed with the list the minister promptly went to the local court and swore out a plea for a trial. The inevitable train of events was set in motion and Jonet was duly arrested and locked up in the tolbooth.

Already weak from lack of food and in pain from arthritis, it took only a couple of days of being watched, walked and questioned before Jonet could take no more and confessed her crime. Yes, she was a witch, had renounced her baptism and made a pact with Auld Nick. One of the beliefs prevalent at the time was that on renunciation of their Christian baptism, a new witch would place one hand on their head and, hopping on one leg, grasp the sole of their foot with the other and promise the Devil everything that lay between. Jonet was noted to be so old and crippled that she could barely stand on her two legs, never mind one. However, this appeared to hold little sway with the elders. Now a self-confessed witch, Jonet could only wait for her trial which was set for three days hence. The Kirk elders and the Commissioners prepared their case. The local executioners started to gather wood. A guilty verdict and execution was the most likely outcome; however, the Devil, no doubt taking care of one of his own, had other plans and, at some point over the following two days, old Jonet died. Her death was most likely due to the combination of old age, illness and poor treatment in gaol but was taken by the authorities of 'proof' of her guilt and was recorded as the 'death of a known witch'.[71]

The records do not state what happened to Jonet's body but although not formally convicted, no Kirk burial appears to have taken place. Her name does not appear on any Kirk burial register. She may have received a pauper's burial but despite the lack of trial she had been labelled witch and it is more likely that her body would have been dumped. As taking her out to the hills or moorland outside the town would have involved time and effort, it is more likely her body was merely cast into the Gala water. Regardless of the fact that there had not been an actual trial, all six Commissioners claimed expenses for their time interrogating Jonet Armstrong. They each received £5 Scots for their trouble from the public purse. During the time of her imprisonment and interrogation, one shilling and sevenpence was spent on bread and ale for Jonet. Her petticoats, which had so offended the minister, were sold for washing rags to pay the bill for her bread.

Before the Reformation, the prosecution of witches along with other matters of morality was a matter for the church with the secular authorities playing a more minor role. After the Reformation, however, the General Assembly of the Kirk was concerned with the entire area of social control and how this should be administered. They were, after all, building God's new society. The chaos that had reigned during the wars of the Reformation may have been, for the most part, behind them, but the Kirk was under no illusion that the Devil would attack the new faith in whatever manner he could. The morality of the common people was ripe for exploitation unless the authorities took firm control. The Kirk wrote to the Privy Council suggesting that either the Kirk take over the jurisdiction of such matters or that the Privy Council undertake to do so. Witchcraft was not specifically outlined but, either way, the Kirk wanted social control firmly embedded in the legislation of the new nation of God.

When the new criminal law was drafted in 1563, witchcraft was listed as an area for the secular authorities. However, the legislation was poorly drafted and the Kirk pushed for greater clarity on the matter. After several years of intense pressure, in 1567, the Parliament debated how 'witchcraft sal be puneist and inquisition takin thereof'.[72]

As far as the Kirk was concerned, they were the lead authority in witchcraft cases with the secular courts merely the instrument by which punishment was meted out. This attitude was not challenged by the Privy Council. In 1575, the Kirk outlined its powers with regard to witchcraft: 'the Kirk hath power to cognosce and decerne upon heresies, blasphemie, witchcraft and violation of the Sabbath day without prejudice always of the civill punishment'.[73] Yet again the Privy Council made no reply to this statement.

During the 17th century, the power and influence of the Kirk in the secular courts was further consolidated by the passing of the Act of Classes and the Test Act. In 1649, the Act of Classes was passed which gave the Kirk in Scotland a veto over those allowed to hold office, including court officials. Those who did not bow to the authority of the Kirk would simple not gain a position. Then in 1681, the Test Act was passed, which required any person holding office to acknowledge the supremacy of the Kirk of Scotland. Initially brought in to bar Roman Catholics from public office, it was worded such that it could be argued that the Kirk had supremacy in all court cases involving issues of morality. What it meant in reality was that the Kirk had complete control over witchcraft trials and could not be challenged.

The courts that prosecuted witches might be secular but that was merely a legal technicality and it was the Kirk that would determine both guilt and punishment. The implementation of this became the established custom and practice throughout central and lowland Scotland. The Highland and Islands had the practices and customs of the clan system with loyalties more likely to be given to the clan chief than a distant Kirk in Edinburgh. Moreover, the retention of Catholic, and older pagan beliefs, in the Highlands and Islands created a different attitude towards witches and how to deal with them.

The result in central and lowland Scotland was that in most trials, guilty verdicts and executions were the norm. In addition, in some cases where the legal niceties had not been fully observed, the secular court authorities would ignore such technicalities and simply yield to the Kirk's rule.

To bring a suspected witch to trial involved a somewhat complicated legal process. Firstly, a complaint had to be raised and the suspected witch identified. Then the decision would be taken whether or not to try the accused. Following receipt of the correct legal permissions to try the suspect, the witch would be arrested and interrogated. After interrogation, the accused would either be released or finally brought to trial. Unless the accused died in gaol, very few suspected witches were not brought to trial after interrogation. On the few occasions this did happen, it was usually where the accused was male or wealthy or well-connected and would challenge the accusation.

The whole process would usually start with a complaint from an individual who suspected that some event in their lives, an illness or a business failure, was the result of the actions of a witch. The individual would then usually go to the Kirk minister and complain. At this point, the minister would decide whether or not to investigate further. (There are no recorded cases where a complaint to a minister did not result in an investigation.) If he so decided, this was followed by a formal request to the Privy Council in Edinburgh, the Committee of Estates or the Parliament for a Commission of Justiciary to try a witch which allowed the minister to mount an investigation, at the end of which a decision would be made as to whether or not to proceed to trial. If the Commission, under the guidance of the minister, sought a trial, they would go to the requisite court and lodge a formal request for trial under the terms of the Commission.

The complexity of this process makes the numbers involved in witchcraft trials even more astonishing as, theoretically, at any point in the chain, the process could be halted. There are no records showing how many initial complaints that were lodged failed to result in a full trial. However, the role of the Kirk in the process tended to ensure that once an initial complaint was laid it almost inevitably led to a trial. Once the minister had been told of an offence and been given a name, it was he who guided the Commission in its investigations to produce the evidence on which the court decided whether or not to hold a trial. There was also one other crucial role early in the process which fell to the minister. Not every individual who complained about being the victim of witchcraft named a specific witch. A general complaint of suspected witchcraft may have been made when a child was ill or food had been spoiled without the victim being absolutely sure of the perpetrator. In these cases, it would be the minister who would supply the name.

For a witchcraft case, the minister might decide who the accused was, would list the offences against the accused, carry out an initial investigation, lead the interrogation after the accused's formal arrest, plead for a trial and then present the evidence against the accused witch in court. The minister had several other areas of influence. The local magistrates called to run the Commission, the 'guid men', were usually selected on the recommendation of the minister but also the character witnesses brought in to testify against the witch's character were usually selected on the grounds of their honesty as judged by the minister. Within the process, ministers were permitted to go out looking for witnesses to support the initial accusation. The jury selection was based on the grounds of an honest and godly character as recommended by the minister. These would, obviously, be members of the minister's own congregation and unlikely to give a verdict of innocent as the original accusation came from their own spiritual leader. Even if a member of the jury had doubts about the accused's guilt, the repercussions to the individual, especially in small, close knit communities, were such that most remained silent.

The court system for cases of witchcraft involved several different types of courts, all of which had their own specialised roles. From the first complaint to the passing of sentence on a convicted witch could involve more than one court at different stages of the proceedings.

The first court was that of the local Kirk sessions and Presbyteries. Although the Kirk had the authority to gather evidence, they did not have any criminal jurisdiction and once a case was prepared against a suspect it would be passed onto either the Sheriff Courts; Burgh Courts; local Criminal Courts; Circuits Courts; or Court of Justiciary. The Kirk, depending on the severity of the case, would apply to the Privy Council, the Committee of Estates or the Parliament to ask for a Commission of Justiciary. This was the formal authority necessary in order for an interrogation and trial to be held. Once a Commission was granted, formal interrogation could begin and a trial could proceed. Although the Kirk session had the right to investigate allegations, it did not have the right to interrogate suspects or use torture until a Commission had been issued. Before the 17th century, the issuing of a Commission was not a routine procedure. The issuing authority, usually the Privy Council, had to have a reasonable understanding that there was a case to answer. By the 17th century, the increased numbers of requests for Commissions was such that the rigour of the authorities in checking there was a case to answer lessened and many Commissions were routinely granted if the minster who had applied was known to be of good character. Commissions could vary in what they allowed local investigators to do. Some explicitly stated that torture could be used; some expressly forbade torture. Some gave local investigators a wide remit of who they could interrogate; yet others placed limits on the powers of the Commission in terms of time and geographical spread.

The Sheriff Courts and Burgh Courts were the normal local courts which dealt with local crime. As witchcraft was considered a serious crime, it was usually considered to be beyond their normal jurisdiction and rarely came before them. There are, however, some cases of witch trials coming before the Sheriff courts in the Borders. It is unclear from the records exactly why this was but it may well have been a matter of expediency as the local Sheriff courts would have dealt quickly with local cases and sent the guilty to the flames. They might also have been less scrupulous with the tedious application of legal technicalities which could frustratingly slow proceedings down. The Sheriff courts could conveniently ignore situations in which torture had been applied in contradiction of the terms of the original Commission. Local criminal courts were held under the Commissions of Justiciary that were issued. Most Scottish witchcraft trials were held in local criminal courts. These were generally convened to try one individual. These courts were most common in urban areas. Circuit Courts held the same authority as the Court of Justiciary and travelled round the country to areas where no other suitable court existed to try witch cases. This court was most common in rural areas and carried out the greatest number of trials in the Borders. The Court of Justiciary itself was the highest criminal court in the land and was situated in Edinburgh. The Circuit Courts relied on the local nobility to act as Commissioners in witchcraft cases.

The process between initial accusation and final sentence could be a long and arduous one.

The Kirk took its work most seriously and proceeded slowly and methodically, investigating and gathering evidence over a prolonged period of time. Once they were convinced of the guilt of the individual, they then applied for a Commission to try the witch; that in itself could take time. Not only was communication slow, especially in the winter months, but the Privy Council often took some time deciding upon each Commission application. There were also other duties to be performed by the Privy Council and, despite the insistence of the Kirk, not every Commission application was a priority. The Privy Council might also ask for further evidence to be gathered which further prolonged matters. This usually happened, not because the Council was concerned about the veracity of the case, but because of local politics. In-fighting between noble families was rife and a word in the right ear could allow the Privy Council to demand more detail in a particular case. This show of central power served to undermine the authority of one local family to the advantage of another.

Once a Commission had been granted then further time was spent gathering the Circuit Court Commissioners. In rural areas, where life was dominated by the agricultural year, individuals were frequently not available at busy times such as during spring sowing and harvest. Once the Commissioners were free then the real interrogations could begin. Depending on what evidence had been gathered by the minister's initial investigations, the interrogation of suspected witches, the rounding up other suspects and their subsequent interrogation could take come considerable time.

Once a trial took place, however, the proceedings could progress relatively quickly. Most witnesses that had to be called lived locally. There was one problem with witnesses: in 16th century Scotland, women did not exist as far as criminal law was concerned. They were considered the equivalent of children and could not be called to give evidence in a trial.

My Lord Advocat alleadged that... no woman cane be witnes because by the uncontraverted laes and pract'qs of Scotland.[74]

This inability of women to give evidence posed a problem for the courts dealing with witchcraft cases. Most of the initial accusations had come from women but their evidence would be inadmissible in the courts. Even more troubling was the fact that one of the main proofs against an individual was to be named by another witch. However, as most witches were women, their evidence would also be inadmissible. Other proofs and evidence were acceptable but the inability to introduce the fact that one witch had named another worried the authorities. It was well known that a witch could, on occasions, hide her Devil's mark. What if the witch by using some devilish trickery tampered with the other evidence against them in a trial? Without the evidence of delation by another witch, some cases might fall. As the number of witchcraft trials rose so too did the concern that some witches would escape their punishment. As the 17th century beckoned, this problem was solved by the passing of a Parliamentary Act in 1591 that allowed women to give testimony in court, but only in a case involving witchcraft.

Trials were also rapid due to the lack of any defence case. The particular nature of witchcraft trials and the fact that the prosecution case was led by the local minister rendered a defence case difficult. To defend a witch was in effect to call the local minister a liar. It was quite simply unthinkable. Some argued that, as a witch's power came from the Devil, it was by its very definition indefensible. In addition, in many instances advocates in the Borders were related to the members of the Commission or the elders and minister of the Kirk involved in a trial. Family loyalty would mitigate offering to defend an accused witch. Even where a defence could be mounted, the cost of an advocate was usually well outwith the pocket of most Borderers. In the trials where a defence was offered, it was usually in cases of members of the middling classes or nobility.

The Scottish 'Poor's Roll' came into being in 1424. This stated that 'and gif there bee onie pure creature, for faulte of cunning, or expenses, that cannot, nor may not follow his cause, the King for the love of GOD, sall ordain the judge to purwey and get a leill and a wise Advocate, to follow sik pure creatures causes.'[75] In 1587, the Scots Parliament passed an act that gave

> quhatsumever lieges of this Realme accused of treason, or for quatsumever crime… full libertie to provide himselfe of Advocates and Praeloquutoures, in competent numbers to defend his life, honour and land, against quhatsumever accusation.[76]

The legal profession accepted these tenets as a duty to offer free legal assistance to poor prisoners. However, due to the authority of the Kirk and their dominant role in witchcraft cases, the legal requirement on the authorities to protect an individual by providing a defence advocate was challenged. The Kirk argued that the nature of the crime of witchcraft was such that those prisoners were outwith the normal moral sphere and as such did not deserve the assistance of an advocate. The robustness of this stance was such that, in almost all witchcraft cases involving the poor, there was no defence.

A person could be acquitted, found guilty or found not proven on some or all charges. In the case of being found guilty, sentence depended on the severity of the crime but also the influence of the local Kirk. Most courts recognised that while the actions of a witch were criminal, the causes of witchcraft were spiritual and fell into the authority of the Kirk. Naturally when sentence was to be passed, they turned to the Kirk for guidance. Sentence could be excommunication, banishment or exile, branding, death by burning or, as more regularly happened, death by strangulation and then burning. All witches were excommunicated, although this could be for a short period of time in some instances. Some witches, mainly those with money and influential friends, managed to be exiled. Most Kirk ministers and elders, however, followed their scripture's command of 'thou shalt not suffer a witch to live'. While it was the legal responsibility of the court to pass sentence, the command of the Kirk as moral guardian was, in almost all cases, absolute. It was rare for a court not to follow the Kirk's command and where this happened it was usually in the case of a wealthy and influential individual. Most witches were worriet then burned.

The Condemnatory Acts

Between 1640 and 1649, five separate Condemnatory Acts against witches were passed by the Kirk Assembly.[77] Each act became more censorious, culminating in the 1649 Act which named individuals tasked to deal with the issue. Even in the years where no acts were passed, the problem of witchcraft was still debated by the assembly with the declaration that all measures should be employed against the growing evil. The assembly debates considered what measures should be introduced against witches, how to recognise witchcrafts and called on greater co-operation between authorities against witches. The assembly did not debate the existence of witches and witchcraft, both of which were considered self-evident.

The first Condemnatory Act 1640

The Assembly ordaines all ministers within the kingdome, carefully to take notice of charmers, witches, and all such abusers of the people, and to urge the acts of Parliament to be execute against them; and that the commissioners from the Assembly to the Parliament shall recommend to the said supreme judicatory the care of the execution of the lawes against such persons in the most behoovefull way.

The last Condemnatory Act 1649

The Generall Assembly, taking to their serious consideration the growth of the sins of witchcraft, charming, and consulting, notwithstanding the frequent recommendations for restraining thereof, and remembring that the Generall Assembly, 1647, did propose a good way for the tryall and punishment of these sinnes, by appointing conferences with some ministers, lawyers, and physitians in that matter, which hath never yet taken effect; therefore, the Assembly doth appoint Masters Robert Dowglas, Robert Blair, Mungo Law, James Hammilton, John Smith, Robert Traill, George Leslie, John Hamilton, John Duncan, Samuel Rutherfoord, James Wood, John Leviston, James Guthrie, Andro Cant, David Calderwood, John Moncreiff, Frederick Carmichael, James Durhame, Patrick Gillespie, Robert Ker, Ephraim Melvill, ministers, to consider seriously of that matter, and to consult and advise therein amongst themselves, as also with Sir Archbald Johnston of Wariston, Clerk-Register, Mr Thomas Nicolson, his Majesty's Advocate, Mr Alexander Pierson, one of the Ordinary Lords of Session, Sir Lewes Stewart, Mr Alexander Colvill, and Mr James Robertson, Justice-Deputes, Masters Rodger Mowet, John Gilmoir, and John Nisbet, lawyers; and with Doctors Sibbald, Cunninghame, and Purves, physitians, severally or together, as occasion shall offer. And the Assembly earnestly requests, and confidently expects, from these learned and judicious lawyers and physitians beforenamed, their best endeavours and concurrence with their brethren of the ministrie, for advise and counsell herein, and for conference in the said matter; and ordaine the said brethren to make report of the result of their consultations and conferences from time to time, as they make any considerable progresse, to the Commission for Publick Affaires; and the said Commission shall make report to the next Generall Assembly.

In effect, the Condemnatory Acts consolidated and strengthened the existing act of 1573, extending it to tackle those who dealt with 'Devils and familiar spirits' and that such persons should be put to death.

11

Jedburgh, 1671

'ane sterving conditione'

LYING JUST TEN miles north of the border between Scotland and England, Jedburgh had seen its fair share of destruction in the wars with the English in the 16th century as well as the cross-border raids of the reivers. It was also the site of the infamous Jethart Justice when men were hanged first and tried after. By the time the 17th century arrived, it had, however, settled down into a more peaceable town, with trade starting to flourish as a result of the fertile surrounding farmland and aided by roads both north and south. But just like the other Borders towns it was not to escape the scourge of the Covenanters' wars, plague and harvest failure. Neither was it free from the witchcraft trials. By the 1670s, the Covenanters had mostly put away their swords and the Kirk had settled its differences with kings and parliaments. Famine lay over 20 years in the past and the town breathed a little easier. A perfect time for the old enemy to strike again. This was to provide a new twist to Jethart Justice.

In the early spring of 1671, Mary Sommerveil and Andrew Laidly of Jedburgh were delated as witches, arrested and placed in the tolbooth of Jedburgh.[78] In the April, the pair were seen at the Circuit Court in Jedburgh which found a case against them and sent the papers up to the High Court of Justiciary in Edinburgh for Sommerveil and Laidly to be tried for the crime of witchcraft. However, in July, their case was dismissed by the High Court as there was no evidence against them and no witnesses against them. In the case of Mary, the High Court stated 'that ther was no informatione given in against her nor persone compeiring to insist against her... ordaines the petitioner to be put at libertie.'[79] But this triumph of justice leaves several questions unanswered. How could there be no witness against Mary when she had been delated, who had delated her and why had the Jedburgh Circuit Court sent her case of Edinburgh?

Mary Sommerveil is recorded as being delated as a witch, not accused. So, whoever had called her witch was themselves a witch. Had she been delated by Andrew Laidly? Puzzlingly, the name of the accusing witch is not listed. Neither is the name of who delated Andrew recorded. A quarrel with a spiteful neighbour could have given rise to an accusation of witchcraft sufficient to cause the initial arrest but that was a very different thing from being delated by another witch. Have the records been lost? However, no witness appeared against either accused, which somewhat contradicts them having been delated; the original witch that delated them being just such a witness.

But the case of Mary and Andrew was followed just a matter of weeks later by another where the authorities in Edinburgh became involved and ordered the release of a suspected warlock, George Guislet. As in the first case, George had been arrested after having been delated as a warlock but yet again the records state there were no witnesses against him. George was released in July 1671, just one week after Mary and Andrew, under the orders of the Justiciary Court of Edinburgh. The court records: 'George Guislet imprisoned for witchcraft at the last circuit at Jedburgh is sett at liberty because none compears to insist'.[80] And again the questions arise: why was a case found against George when no witnesses existed? The two cases do not seem to have been connected but, with three arrests in Jedburgh with no witnesses or evidence, the questions simply multiply. What was going on in Jedburgh?

With no witnesses or evidence against the three suspects, there was only one authority that had the power to order an arrest in such a case: the Kirk. An unsupported accusation from a neighbour might have quickly sparked an investigation but with no evidence or witnesses would have equally rapidly been dismissed. Most records of petty squabbles between neighbours show just that outcome with the accuser often chided for their ill temper by the local minister. In some instances, cases were brought against accusers for slander where the word witch had been uttered. For Mary, Andrew and later George to land in the tolbooth without any witnesses against them could only mean the original accusation emanated from the Kirk.

Arrested, probably, on the word of the minister, Mary and Andrew sat for four months in gaol while the local authorities tried to find some evidence against them. No witness came forward. Was 'delated' inserted into the records in order to 'beef up' the charges? With no evidence to substantiate the accusation, the elders could have called in a witch brodder to brod for the Devil's mark but never did. If Mary and Andrew been such powerful witches that no one dared confront them but the minister, that would account for the lack of witnesses. But in such a situation, the natural course of action would have been to bring in a witch brodder. The reluctance of the elders to do so further supports the idea that the initial and only accusation against Mary and Andrew came from the minister; an accusation that could not even persuade the elders to call in a witch brodder.

The Jedburgh records do not state what crimes Mary and Andrew were alleged to have committed, it only states they were 'accused of witchcraft'.[81] None of the usual accusations of causing illness or ruining crops were recorded. As a result of the lack of evidence against them, Mary and Andrew had no trouble in finding an advocate to draw up a petition for their release. The papers for Mary's release, signed in July, state that she was in 'ane sterving conditione'.[82] Andrew, it seems, was also in a poor state. It may be that the cost of an advocate had swallowed up what little money they had, leaving none for food. Whatever the cost of the advocate, it seemed money well spent when he petitioned the court in Edinburgh for Mary and Andrew's release. The petition clearly stated the lack of evidence against the two and their willingness to appear before any court to answer for the charges against them. The appeal reached the Privy Council in Edinburgh who demanded to see the case papers.

The which day anent ane petitione presented to his majisties justices be Marie Somervail prisoner with in the tolbuith of Jedburgh make and mentione that wher the petitioner being caleit befor them at Jedburgh for the crym of witchcraft aleadgit comited, be her, wher upon she was in carcerat and put in prisone and lyen even since in ane sterving conditione.[83]

Whatever was in the case papers, not all of the records of the case have survived, it was sufficient for the authorities in Edinburgh to order the pair's immediate release from gaol. They were released with the stipulation that they hold themselves ready to appear before the court in Edinburgh at any time if so called. 'Mary Sommerveil and Andre Laidly both delated of witchcraft sett at liberty upon their petitions in regard none compeared to inform against them, that they enact themselves when called.'[84] Unsurprisingly, the court in Edinburgh never called Mary or Andrew to account as the entire case against them appeared to emanate from one individual, most likely the local Kirk minister, who had called them witches with nothing to substantiate the accusation. The stipulation that they 'enact themselves when called' may well have been the result of the initial accusation having been made by a minister. Although no witnesses had come forward, the accusation from a member of the Kirk might have been sufficient to suggest that the courts continue to watch over Mary and Andrew.

The case of George Guislet followed the same pattern. Edinburgh was again in no doubt there was no case to answer and ordered Jedburgh to release George. 'George Guislet imprisoned for witchcraft at the last circuit at Jedburgh is sett at liberty because none compears to insist.' In George's case, the authorities did not even keep the slightest interest in the case after his release as they did not even ask him to keep himself available. There is no record of George appealing against his imprisonment so it may be he owed his release to Mary and Andrew's determination to clear their names. Had the curious nature of Mary and Andrew's case alerted the authorities in Edinburgh to the possibilities of irregularities in Jedburgh? Had Mary and Andrew been less determined in their fight to clear their names, all three might have fallen victims to Jethart Justice.

A strong personality can be a double-edged sword and it may well have been Mary and Andrew's strong nature that had riled the local minister against them in the first place. Be that as it may, they were released, albeit grudgingly by the authorities in Jedburgh, and disappeared from the official records.

The name of the minister in this case is unknown. The records do not show any investigation into the Jedburgh authority's illegal imprisonment of Mary, Andrew and George or the role of that local minister and Kirk elders. Perhaps they have been lost, or perhaps the Edinburgh authorities, while willing to act when compelled by an advocate, left well alone where Jethart Justice was concerned.

The aftermath of a witch trial was a tense time in many communities. Once the excitement of the trial was over and the guilty had been duly disposed of, life in the community was supposed to return to normal. The court had left or been dissolved. But the community was often left with a series of unsettling questions. The witch was dead but did more lurk in unsuspecting corners? Had every witch been caught? If the Devil had attacked previously, why assume he could not attack again? Anxiety, heightened by the recent trial, could give rise to a further round of accusations. Many of the trials in the Borders were followed up a year or two later by a further round of accusation as memories of those who had associated with the executed witch were revived prompted by further illness or when the harvest failed.

In the case of an acquittal, the accused almost always returned to a less than welcoming community. Most were known to the Kirk having been in trouble on more than one occasion before their arrest. Already outcast possibly due to a sharp tongue and definitely after an accusation of witchcraft and a spell in the tolbooth, most would find themselves free but destitute. Several parish records tell the fate of those witches released after paying fines or even those acquitted but still suspected in their communities. Homes left weeks previously in exchange for gaol were no longer welcoming and those without family to support them often found themselves homeless.

Even those with a family frequently found themselves turned out of the family home. Unable to get work due to their reputation or to do any work due to the after-effects of the torture that they had endured in gaol, they would soon turn to begging. Initially, fear of retribution arising from a refusal to help a suspected witch would earn them a crust from most but, as summer turned to autumn and autumn to winter, food and shelter would become increasingly scarce. A Borders winter spent out of doors with little or no food and shelter would test the strongest of constitutions, let alone someone who had spent time in gaol having undergone torture and ill treatment. Even for those able to stay in their communities, the welcome was far from warm. Acquitted by the courts was one thing but suspected by your neighbours of having 'got off' by some diabolical means was quite another. Fear would keep most individuals away from the 'witch' but muttered suspicion would feed distrust on one side and resentment on the other and, when any disaster struck again, a further round of accusations and arrests could be expected. Many records show the same names recurring time and again with the same individuals having records that stretch over 20 years. In some extreme cases, local communities took matters into their own hands and those suspected were lynched or stoned to death.

Flitting to another village or town was rarely an option but even when it was tried the results were seldom much better. Moving from a known, even if hostile, environment to an unknown one was a daunting task. Few people moved around in 17th century Borders and those that did tended to move from villages to the nearest town where they would generally be known. Movement of farm goods to markets ensured that anyone attempting to escape a bad reputation would most likely be seen by someone from their hometown or village. Once named as a witch, the new town would view an incomer with double suspicion: now known as a 'witch', they could only have moved for one reason – to practise witchcraft. Any out of the ordinary occurrence, any illness, and the incomer was the first name on everyone's lips.

But it was not just an acquitted witch who faced challenges. Doubts could also arise over the recent conviction. Had those that had died really been guilty? No one could voice any doubts, as this would, by implication, cast doubt on the initial accusation and reputation of the minister. For all that individuals in the 17th century believed in the existence of witches, they were not stupid. The fact that some people were liars, some took advantage of situations and others acted out of malice was not unknown. After witchcraft trials, villages and towns had to attempt to regain some semblance of community but when the guilty witch had been generally known and liked, their execution was hard to reconcile with previous memories of friendship or neighbourliness. This was especially so when the witch had recanted their confession.

And what of the accusers? For the weeks of the investigation and trial, their place within the community had altered dramatically. For a brief time, all of the local men of authority – the minister, the Kirk elders, the sheriff, the baillie and, even in some cases, the local laird – had treated them with respect. They had status and public approval. Indeed, they had power. After the trial and execution, however, the community and their place within it reverted back to normal. The thrill and excitement of being the centre of attention was replaced with the mundane life of rural work. For some, this was a difficult transition and in some of the records in the Borders, a few individuals reappear levelling accusations of witchcraft on numerous occasions. It could be that they genuinely believed that their continued misfortune was the result of witches or they could have found the lure of the excitement of being the victim and accuser of witches too appealing. For those who had made accusations, there were other long-term effects. They had indeed done their duty: they had consigned a witch to eternal damnation but that could prove a burden. For most ordinary people, hell was not a great theological concept but a real place – a place that you might well go to when you died. For those who attended the Kirk, they were reminded of this fact in almost every weekly sermon. Didn't the minister explain in detail the torments awaiting those who denied God? Belief in hell was universal. Hell was a place of everlasting torment; a place of pain and unimaginable suffering that went on for all eternity. And this was the place to which they had consigned the witches. Even those of the strongest constitution might have cause for some reservations at their actions, especially when most witch accusations were made against a neighbour that may have previously been a friend.

There was also the problem that many believed that the witch had not quite died and gone to hell. Although local ministers forced almost total attendance at witch execution and everyone had seen the strangling and burning, it was known that witches had special powers. Had they really died or had they turned themselves into a crow and flown away at the last minute, leaving behind only their human body? The Kirk strove to dismiss such beliefs but these old ideas were deeply rooted and could easily resurface in the events of more cases of witchcraft. In some Borders communities, accusations were made against witches that had previously been executed.

Dead witches could, it seemed, return to torment people in the night. Those who claimed to have been hag-ridden in the night (ridden by a hag or witch while asleep) would equally accuse a witch long-dead as one alive. But even if a witch was really dead and had been sent to hell, this often gave little comfort. After the trial of a witch, many were seen to attend the Kirk most assiduously for several weeks but the minister could often not calm the fears of his parishioners. If hell was where individuals were sent when they were evil and denied God, how was that a punishment for witches who had already denied God? If hell was the withdrawal of God's grace, why would witches fear hell when they had already rejected God's grace? And how could witches fear hell if it was presided over by Auld Nick, their master? Furthermore, if hell was ruled by the Devil then what was to stop him sending his witches out of hell back to Earth to torment people? The Kirk could not answer and could not reassure. Many ministers attempted to calm these fears by telling their communities not to ask such questions and to merely trust in the Lord. This merely confused and frustrated communities and did nothing to abate their fear. With no answers coming from the Kirk and with witches still abroad in the Borders, ordinary people would often fall back into the very superstition of witchcraft by using charms and amulets to protect themselves.

But there were still other more mundane tensions that arose. Witchcraft trials disrupted community life. The normal business of a village or town was upset as individuals were taken from their usual tasks to guard witches or act on the jury. Timber and other supplies were diverted to the court and strangers arrived that needed fed and housed along with their horses. The trial also saw money exchange hands; at least for some. Certain individuals who had given evidence may have profited as a piece of land had come their way or been awarded compensation for a dead pig by the courts, but that too could have its downside. Resentment came from those who had been equally affected by the witch but had not gained in any way. There were also those who had not been witnesses but had still been seen to profit. The usual ones had had their snouts in the trough selling coal and tar to burn the witch, providing food and lodgings to the courts and their officials. Of those involved in the trial and in providing supplies, not all were paid with equal speed. Resentments simmered under the surface of those who were out of pocket. In the few cases where suspects were acquitted, the non-payment of bills was especially resented. The non-payment of services to some individuals in a community while the accused witch walked free caused a considerable degree of bitterness.

Another source of tension was found in those families who had lost a mother, a wife, a sister. They had to rebuild their lives. Those that had abandoned the witch to her fate were left with the guilt of having failed in their duty to a loved one. Those who had managed to stand by their relative faced disapproval and condemnation from the Kirk and community alike. Tainted by association, suspicion could become lodged in a neighbour's mind. Even for those whose relation had died due to torture or ill treatment in gaol, or who had simply been unable to withstand their treatment and had committed suicide, the accusation of witch stuck. When ill-fortune struck the community again, voices muttered and old tales were revived. Was this an attack from new witches or was it the revenge of the family of the old witch that had been put to death? A witch's child might easily grow up to be a witch themselves or might already be one. What powers might they have, what revenge might they wreak and on whom?

A witchcraft trial had one last gift to bestow on the community: fear. The Devil had attacked them before, he could attack them again at any minute. No longer could illness be viewed as natural; it was forevermore to be seen as the work of diabolical witches. The world was a frightening place where witches attacked the godly and threatened their children. The minister in his pulpit had become a more terrifying figure, ever-warning of the dangers of witches and witchcraft and ever-accusing, but offering no answers or succour. Not all witch executions sat well with communities and after the dust had settled more sober heads prevailed. How could an argument over bread have led to a burning? The executed had been known, had been ordinary. If they could be accused, so could anyone. Communities that had seen a trial were uneasy places in the immediate aftermath. Free from witches they might have been but suspicion, resentment and fear had been left in their place.

The frozen body of an emaciated woman, reputed to be that of Mary Sommerveil, was found on 23 December 1671 on the road south out of Jedburgh. As a witch, even one only suspected of witchcraft, she would not be given Christian burial in the Kirkyard. Burial by the road was thought to bring ill luck to travellers and no one was found willing to do the task. The body was stripped and dumped in the Jed Water.

12

Stobo, 1679

'the dumb man in the correction house'

THE LANDS OF Stobo changed hands between the Kirk and the nobility many times from the start of the Reformation until the 17th century. The beginning of the 17th century saw the lands given by James VI first to Sir John Maitland of Thirlestane, then the Duke of Lennox and then in 1608 to the Archbishop of Glasgow. In 1613, the Archbishop granted the lands in a charter to James Tweedie. The lands then passed into the ownership of John Murray of Halmyre in 1619 and Stobo was to remain Murray land for the next 72 years.

Lying just five miles from Peebles, Stobo benefitted from the good pasture, clean water and fair roads to Edinburgh and the west. Stobo, unlike most other Borders towns and villages had experienced very few witchcraft accusations in the 17th century. In the autumn of 1679, a curious case arose where two men from Stobo would be brought to trial not for being warlocks but for the equally heinous crime of having consulted with one. The Witchcraft Act of 1563 was quite specific: it outlawed both witches and those who consulted with witches. The central belief of the Kirk was that a witch had renounced her baptism and made a covenant with the Devil. By consulting with a known witch, an individual was therefore condoning that act and by seeking help from a servant of Auld Nick, rather than from a servant of God, was challenging God's authority. In the eyes of the law and the Kirk, any such individual was an apostate and equally as guilty as any witch.

William and James Stewart were brothers and indwellers of Stobo where they worked as merchants trading farm produce to Peebles and Biggar. Some time in October 1678, they decided to visit a warlock; the dumb man in Edinburgh. This was no drunken spree or spur of the moment decision to visit a local witch but rather a rational and planned act. The brothers had to leave their business, travel to Edinburgh, pay for food and overnight lodgings, pay for stabling for their horses and pay to see the dumb man – no small undertaking and certainly outwith the pocket of most people at that time. In addition, this was not an isolated act. As was to become clear during the investigation into the brothers' activities, this visit to Edinburgh was merely the latest consultation they had undertaken over a period of several months. It is not known what witches other than the dumb man the brothers had consulted. However, as the brothers had not been absent from Stobo for any prolonged period prior to their Edinburgh visit, it may be assumed that the other witches were local. Whatever knowledge or assistance the brothers were seeking, the local witches had been unable to deliver and they sought help from the notorious dumb warlock.

The dumb man is not named in the records but is listed as a 'known warlock'. For some reason, even as a known warlock he had not been executed but was held in a house of correction. If he had been a warlock he should, at the very least, have faced prison, if not execution. However, the description of him as the 'dumb man' may have saved his life. Unable to speak, he had been classed as a lunatic and imprisoned for life in the lunatic asylum; the correction house. It is not known why he could not speak and it may be that this was feigned as a means of escaping execution as a warlock. His inability, or unwillingness, to speak may also have contributed to his reputation as a warlock. The ability to listen to an individual's problems, read signs in water or animal entrails and produce an amulet that would rectify a situation do not necessarily require speech. A mute warlock that still appeared to do magic might appear even more powerful. Whatever the truth of the situation, his fame was such that it drew the Stewart brothers from Stobo to Edinburgh to visit him.

The dumb man may possibly have been allowed some visitors from time to time such as family members, if he had any, but for two strangers to visit would not normally have been allowed. Why would anyone other than a family member or friend want to visit a known warlock who could not speak? For William and James to choose to do so was extremely risky. Both brothers leaving Stobo together, and thus leaving their business unattended would, in itself, have seemed somewhat suspicious to their neighbours even without a visit to a warlock. In Edinburgh, the brothers would have had to have paid the wardens for access to the man and this could also have set tongues wagging. The visit would also have had to be planned in advance. It would have required the brothers to know about the dumb man, find a way to visit him, approach the right guard and negotiate a price for the visit without arousing suspicion. It would also, presumably, have required at least a previous trip to Edinburgh by one of the brothers to make such arrangements.

Whatever excuse they had originally used and however careful they had tried to be in Edinburgh, on their return to Stobo the brothers were reported to the minister. Within a day they were called before the minister and Kirk elders to account for their actions. Further investigations around Stobo by the minister and the elders revealed that the brothers had visited and consulted with several witches and charmers over a matter of months and, convinced that there was a case to answer, the minister called for a Commission. What the minister thought about his two parishioner's belief in witches and their ability to deceive him and the elders for several months is not recorded.

The Privy Council was busy over the winter and the Commission was not received until the spring of the next year. The moment the Commission was received, William and James were arrested and interrogated as to their conduct. The interrogation lasted over the spring and into the summer as it gathered information. Finally convinced that had enough to proceed, the Commissioners set a trial date for late September. The indictment dittay lists several offences against each brother 'consulting with witches, charmers and such as have familiar spirites particularly the dumb man in the correction house of Edinburgh'.[85] It was further noted, however, that neither brother had their own familiar spirits and so it was not thought that they were witches themselves.

On 26 September, the trial began and was deserted that very day.[86] William and James were set free. This was not the same as an acquittal but meant that the trial had been abandoned as there was no case to answer. If the evidence collected by the minister was enough to convince the Privy Council of the need for a Commission and the local Commissioners had set a trial date, why suddenly were those same Commissioners of the opposite opinion that there was no case to answer?

While the records that list the date of the trial remain intact and the records that state that the diet had been deserted remain intact, the record of the names of the local Commissioners that decided there was no case to answer have been lost. But whoever they were, they were the only ones with the authority to stop the trial. Over the spring and summer months, William and James had been under arrest but were not detained in any way; this was common for male suspects. They had gone about their normal business and interestingly had not denied their actions in seeking counsel from witches and warlocks. The evidence was, therefore, plain and uncontested; the trial should have been routine.

Stobo was a relatively small town and the Commissioners would have consisted of the local landowners not all of whom would have lived in in the town but may have lived at some distance. The spring and summer were busy times in the rural Borders and large landowners would have been busy with their estates. Few of them would have been involved in the interrogation which would have been led by the minster and the elders. Presented with a request for a trial by the minister, the Commissioners would in all likelihood have signed off on a trial date after only a cursory examination of the evidence relying on the trust in the minster that all was in order. For some, if not all, of the Commissioners, the first opportunity they would have had to examine the evidence in detail and speak to and hear from William and James would have been at the trial. Could William and James have been about to say something that the local Commissioners wanted left unsaid?

The clue may lie with the dumb man in Edinburgh. To visit and consult the dumb man, the brothers must first have been told of his existence and then how to arrange a clandestine visit. This information is extremely unlikely to have come from the minister or the elders. The brothers might have learned from another witch that the dumb man existed but probably not how to pay the guards to allow them to visit. That was the sort of information that could only come from someone rich enough to have visited the dumb man themselves. How had they come by that information? Who had told them? Before their visit to the dumb man, neither William nor James were noted as being absent from Stobo for any prolonged period. Whoever had told them the information they needed for the Edinburgh visit must have lived relatively locally. Did one of the Commissioners arriving in Stobo for the first time in September realise what William and James could say?

During the brothers' arrest and interrogation by the minister and elders, the brothers had been open about their activities, if not the reason for them. They had answered all questions put to them and did not attempt to escape, despite being allowed to remain in their own homes rather than the tolbooth. Over the spring and summer, neither William nor James sought to engage an advocate to defend them. They seem to have gone about their business as normal despite having a potentially life-threatening trial hanging over their heads. They appeared, in other words, completely untroubled by their situation.

The usual sentence for an individual found guilty of consulting with a known witch or warlock was to be worriet and then burned; William and James left court completely exonerated. The papers detailing why the diet was deserted have completely disappeared. When they visited the dumb man in Edinburgh, William and James were middling folk with a reasonable, if modest, income. After the trial, both continued to successfully trade in the town and with several of the local landowners. Within a few short years, both brothers moved to Edinburgh as extremely wealthy merchants.

The execution of a convicted witch was more or less a foregone conclusion. The scriptures admonished 'thou shalt not suffer a witch to live' (Exodus 22:18) and God's Elect followed scripture to the letter. In Scotland, the main method of execution for witches was to be worriet or strangled and then burned. For those who did not meet this gruesome fate, they could be excommunicated, flogged, branded, exiled, hanged and, for some poor unfortunates, they could be burnt alive without the mercy of having been strangled first. The latter fate tended to be reserved for those intransigent individuals who, as well as their acts of witchcraft, refused to ask for forgiveness and revelled in their wickedness. This could also, if rarely, happen when the alleged crime was so offensive that local outrage overtook the legal niceties.

After sentence was passed, a pyre would be built in a public place, such as the local market square, and everyone would be instructed to attend the execution. The pyre usually consisted mainly of wood with some coal and tar used to help the burning. The wood used was always specifically cut for the witch burning as superstition dictated that one who had given up or sold wood for a burning would be haunted by the witch thereafter and have nothing but bad luck. The wood would be cut and stored usually where the witch was being held as no one wanted even to store the wood. Rope and any other materials used would often be brought in from outwith the town. This was partly because such resources were scarce but also to avoid any possible ill luck associated with the witch.

In some cases, the witch would be burned in a tar barrel instead of being tied to a stake. This usually involved tying the dead body of the worriet witch into a barrel half-filled with tar which was then set alight. Local superstition often preferred this method as it was felt that the barrel was a better container and there was less possibility of an escape at the last moment. Most Kirk ministers vehemently opposed this reasoning, explaining to the ignorant mob that the Devil could not defeat God and rescue 'his' witch. Depending on the mood of the mob and the amount of ale consumed, the theological argument was not always completely believed. The low number of barrel burnings was most likely down to the cost of burning a good barrel.

On the morning of the execution, the witch would be roused at dawn. Long hair would be hacked off for ease of strangulation. The witch would then be put in a hair cloth shift which could open up any pre-existing wounds from brodding or torture. The shift was then painted with tar to help with the burning. The witch then had their shoes removed to appear penitent and barefoot before God. Their hands would be bound behind their back and they would then be marched through the town by two of the baillie's men.

Once they had reached the place of execution, the sentence would then be repeated and the local minister would usually preach a sermon reminding the townsfolk of the wickedness of witches and of the damnation and hellfire that awaited them. The executioner then stepped forward. This may have been a local man but in some of the smaller villages would have had to have been fetched in from one of the larger towns. The executioner was frequently a blacksmith or farrier. Farmers or farm workers seldom acted as executioners as it was feared that any ill-luck from association with a witch might be carried on to the farm, causing a bad harvest or sickness in livestock. After a final exhortation from the minister for the witch to confess their sins and beg the Lord's forgiveness, the executioner went to work. Two baillie's men held onto the witch's arms and would force her into a kneeling position. With the witch in the kneeling position and held fast, the executioner would approach. He would then slip a knotted rope over the witch's head and twist it round the neck until it was tight. He might then put one of his knees in the small of the witch's back to get a good purchase or use the witch's bound hands as a resting place for his foot. They often rested their body weight on the witch's bound hands but as she was held fast by the baillie's man, this would pull down on the arms and could break both shoulders, the crunch of the break easily heard by the surrounding crowd. Once in a comfortable position, the executioner would start to twist the rope. Occasionally a small piece of wood would be inserted between the victim's neck and the rope and the wood was then twisted to increase pressure. It could take a few minutes for the witch to die depending on the strength of the executioner, his experience and the amount of 'give' in the rope. Most witches were unconscious within ten to 15 seconds and inexperienced executioners or, in the case of multiple executions, those who were tired, might then suppose the witch to be dead and deliver them onto the pyre or into the tar barrel still alive.

All this time, the witch was facing the assembled throng of people who watched as she was throttled. Those who looked away were noted and duly admonished by the minister. The spectacle was a truly gruesome one. The face would start to swell up and the lips, tips of the ears and nose would take on a blueish tinge as the blood supply was cut off. The eyes would bulge in their sockets and the tongue would protrude from the mouth. There was usually a frothy mucous streaming from both mouth and nostrils and the on lookers would hear the victim choking. Unable to move to aid themselves, the victim's fingers and hands would twist and turn in the ropes, cutting themselves in the process. After the victim was dead, or appeared dead, the body was tied onto the pyre, or into the barrel, and burned. If the victim was not dead and regained consciousness on the fire, this was seen not as evidence that they had not been worriet properly but as a last feeble attempt by the witch to escape justice. The fact that they did not escape was proof of the Devil's abandonment of the witch in her last agonies.

The execution of a witch served a two-fold purpose: it consigned an evil doer to the flames but just as importantly, it served to illustrate to the local populace the power of the true faith and the trickery of Auld Nick. This was a creature who had promised his followers everything their hearts had desired and he had abandoned them like the liar he was. He had been proved false and wicked and had abandoned them to their fate. It was for this reason that Kirk elders required everyone's presence at an execution. This was also pertinent where several witches were executed together. After the death of the first of their colleagues, they were confronted by the falsity of the Devil and called on to witness his treachery. For those who had not confessed, a final demand that they admit their guilt was made.

Costs

Trying and executing witches was an expensive business. Everything from the messenger who had ridden to Edinburgh to ask for permission from the Privy Council to the coal used to burn the witch's dead body had to be paid for by the local community.

Four fathom of thick rope to bind the witch	6 shilling 8 pennies
Coal to burn the witch	25 shillings 6 pennies
Tar barrels in which to burn the witch	12 shillings
Messengers	45 shillings
Executioner	£3 15 shillings
Baillie's men ale	10 shillings
Brodder	£7 10 shillings

Brodder's servant	20 shillings
Stabling for the brodder's horse	35 shillings
Commissioners	£8 12 shillings
Bread and drink for the Commissioners	30 shillings
Paper to record the Commission	2 shillings 9 pennies
Candles for watching witch	15 shillings
Food and bedding for witch	5 shillings

Unfortunately for many communities these costs could prove contentious; especially as some were considered more important than others. The Commissioners and brodder had to be paid. The costs of getting and recording the Commission and trial also had to be paid. No distinction was made between small villages and large towns, all official bills had to be paid. Not every village could afford a plough tax to cover such expense and even where a local tax had been imposed it barely covered all costs. However, once the official costs were paid the other bills were still due. Who would pay the forester who had supplied the wood or the local smith who had provided stabling? Many bills remained unpaid for years. Ill feeling was caused and could remain when some locals were paid while others were not. The estate of a convicted witch was forfeit to the crown and any monies that were forthcoming would initially pay for expenses such as the Commission or clerk's wages in Edinburgh. Little if any of the surplus, if there was one, would be given to the community to pay any outstanding debts. The surplus would be 'donated' to the Kirk instead. In truth most witches had no estate to leave.

However, not everyone sentenced to death went immediately to the flames. A common delaying tactic was for a woman to 'plead her belly', claiming to be pregnant. The hope was that after several months the locals might, after having had to pay for the witch's keep for so long, once what money the witch had was gone, be disposed to merely send her on her way rather than face the expense of an execution. There was also the idea that a few extra months might give time for an appeal for at least a lesser sentence if not the overturning of the original verdict. However, this was a scheme that was fraught with danger and with little chance of success.

For those who were pregnant, there was no guarantee of release and indeed some towns, after having had to pay for the maintenance of a witch for a further six months or so, often vented their anger the only way they could. They dispensed with the 'mercy' of having the witch worriet and she might find herself facing the flames alive and fully conscious. For those who were not expecting, the problem was how to get pregnant before the nine months were up. While there were some who took sexual advantage of those accused of witch-craft they were, in fact, considerably fewer that might be imagined. Most men were too scared of witches and their evil magic to go anywhere near them. Those who were God-fearing were repulsed by them and their wickedness. Those of a less holy nature were still superstitious and subsequently nevertheless genuinely afraid. It was well known that witches could make you impotent or shrivel your manhood. So finding a guard who would take that risk and oblige was not easy. Those male friends and family members who had not fled in fear or disgust might help but had to get past the guards first and then not get caught. Some, no doubt, would have tried but the risk of capture and subsequent punishment as a witch themselves would have made them few and far between.

For those who were expecting, they had to endure their preg-nancy and subsequent childbirth alone in the confines of an unsan-itary cell after having spent months on little food. The level of miscarriages and still births was high, as was the rate of maternal deaths. For those that safely delivered a child, the fate of their baby was not a happy one. The child was removed moments after birth and given into the care of the parish. But what parish wanted the child of a convicted witch in their midst? Indeed, many babies were found to have nowhere to go. Few female friends or relatives were willing to face being further ostracised by their communities for having taken the child in and yet an unclaimed child would die if not cared for. For those children who were taken in, they would grow up a figure of fear and condemnation. Treatment would have been harsh and basic care minimal, such that many would not see their fifth year. For those that survived into adulthood, life was hard. They were, in many cases, excluded from all aspects of nor-mal community life and if the cry of witch was raised again in their town or village, theirs was the first name on everyone's lips.

The Kirk, so eager to condemn the mother, was less enthusiastic in the care of the child. John Knox had introduced parish care for foundlings and orphaned children as part of a Christian duty of care. However, in the case of the children of witches, this Christian duty fell very short of actual care. Children orphaned by the death of a mother and with no family would be placed in the care of a local family and their basic upkeep paid by the Kirk until they were old enough to earn a living at around seven or eight. No such luxury was afforded the child of an executed witch as frequently Kirk funds were not exactly forthcoming. Despite the estate of a witch being forfeit to the Crown, even where monies were left over after the payment of expenses, little appears to have been set aside for the care of any children. It was difficult to find those willing to take in the baby of a witch. Could the baby also be a witch? Could the executed witch have inhabited the body of the baby just before death? Would the Devil appear to claim the child for himself? Would the baby bring bad luck? Despite these fears, there were some willing to take the risk. This was seldom from a sense of Christian duty but more the practical need to make money as some could be prised from the local Kirk funds. Whatever the reason, the babies seldom survived long. Before long, the stress of caring for a child, the expense of another mouth to feed when the Kirk money had dried up or the nagging fear of bad luck would see the baby turned out of the house. Infants were left out on the hills to perish in the cold Borders winter with the remote valleys of the Ettrick and Yarrow waters particularly favoured spots for such an abandonment. An indifferent Kirk did not investigate. Even those babies dying of natural causes were frequently denied Christian burial by the Kirk.

13

Coldingham, 1694

'burn seven or eight of them'

ONE OF THE issues that frequently arises in reading and research-ing about the witchcraft trials, as in many areas of history, is the paucity of records that have survived. Another issue is the vague-ness of the records that do exist. How many trials took place? How many witches were executed? Were any killed illegally? None of these questions can be answered with absolute certainty but a careful reading of what records do exist may give some clues. The town of Coldingham illustrates this.

In September 1629, a Commission was granted to Sir Patrick Home of Aittoun to try David Nisbett in Coldinghame, Margaret Baleny in Ayttoun, Agnes Falconer in Eymouth and Jane Liddell for witchcraft. Later in the same year, a Commission was granted to the sheriff of Berwick to try Helen Huldie in Coldingham for witchcraft. In 1698, Margaret Polwart, Jean Hart and Alison Nisbet were accused of witchcraft. The records for all of these cases give little detail but there is nothing in them that is out of the ordinary. The records of trials in Coldingham are similar to those across other Border towns.

In 1694, however, there is a curious entry. Sir Alexander Home of Renton complained to Lord Polwarth of the great increase in witches in the parish and stated that his father, as sheriff, had at one time 'caused to burn seven or eight of them.'[87] This comment could be dismissed as a casual remark about the lack of rigour in pursuing witches. However, there are a num-ber of instances across the Borders where 'several witches were burned' but no trial records exist. Was this one of those instances? Parish records, local diaries and letters record incidents of witch executions presided over by local ministers and gentry but with no mention of any trials having taken place. Black's Calendar of Witchcraft[88] lists several of these 'executions'. Moreover, these executions always involved several witches. The apparent 'execution' of accused witches without benefit of trial merely shows the level of fear across the Borders that resulted in such actions. In addition to the general fears of the 17th century, there were three reasons particular to Coldingham that may have resulted in an illegal execution: a site of ancient worship, location on the coast and a rather particular Kirk minister.

Coldingham had been the site of Christian worship since the early 7th century when a priory was built. The establishment of the priory at Coldingham could have been chosen for a number of reasons but sites of Christian worship in Scotland were frequently built on sites of previous pagan worship. While this was known, and conveniently ignored, by the early church, it became a major issue at the time of the Reformation. The arrival of the Protestant church in Scotland classed everything that was not Calvinist as 'Devil worship' whether this was an old belief in pagan magic or Catholicism. As far as the local Kirk was concerned, the pagan roots of the common people were lying just below the surface. With the Devil roaming the land in the 17th century, he would easily find followers in such an area. It might seem surprising that the Kirk believed that over 1,000 years of Christian worship could so easily be swept away. However, the strength of the Devil was not in doubt in the Borders and the new Protestant Kirk found Coldingham troublesome. On the one hand, it had been a site of Christian worship for over 1,000 years. On the other, the priory had been founded by a woman, a Catholic saint, St Ethredreda. The matter of Catholic saints, especially female ones, proved to be a thorny theological issue for the Protestant church for many years but in the century after the Reformation, the thought of a holy site founded by a Catholic female was anathema to the Kirk. But in addition to Coldingham's foundation by St Ethredreda, there was the issue of immorality. No less a person than St Cuthbert had, in the 7th century, publicly condemned the monks and nuns of Coldingham for their moral laxity. The Kirk had, therefore, to contend with a holy site founded by a woman, on the probable site of pagan worship that had been previously condemned for immorality. In combination, this made Coldingham fertile ground for witches.

The second reason for Coldingham's focus for witchcraft was its location on the coast. As a coastal town, Coldingham had to deal with the vagaries of the weather and local tides. The coastal waters off the east of Scotland are prone to sudden changes of weather even in the summer months, resulting in unexpected and unexplainable storms that sank fishing boats and ships and caused coastal flooding. Due to the speed at which the weather could change and the inherent dangers of death by drowning, many fishermen were superstitious. Although condemned by the Kirk as pagan nonsense, these superstitions remained. It was bad luck to sail on Thursdays (God of Storms, Thor's day) or Fridays (the day Jesus was executed), as well as the first Monday in April (the day Cain killed Abel), the second Monday in August (the day Sodom and Gomorrah were destroyed) and 31 December (the day on which Judas Iscariot hanged himself). Whistling or singing into the wind was forbidden as it would 'whistle up a storm'. It was also unlucky to set off at the start of the fishing season without having first shed some blood in a fight or in an accident. And when setting fishing nets, it was good luck to use an odd number. Having the caul of a new-born child on board a boat was meant to prevent anyone from drowning. Some words and sayings brought about bad luck on board, including 'drowned', 'goodbye' and 'good luck'. Things to do with the land were believed to be bad luck if mentioned, such as the church, cats and rabbits. It was bad luck for fishermen's wives to call out to them or wave goodbye once they stepped out the door to leave for a voyage. In order to encourage fish to be caught, Scottish fishermen would begin their fishing session by throwing one of the crew members overboard and then hauling him back on. Egg shells had to be broken into tiny pieces once an egg was cracked open. This was meant to stop witches sailing to the ship in the pieces of shell. Despite the best efforts of the Kirk, these superstitions remained even among the most zealous of church-goers. When bad weather prevented fishermen from setting sail or when a boat was caught in a storm, those same individuals might give thanks to the Lord that no one had drowned while at the same time looking for someone to blame for the misfortune. By the 17th century the person to blame was obvious: a witch.

The local minister was the third reason for the situation in Coldingham. All of the Kirk ministers across the Borders were zealous in their pursuit of witches, convinced as they were that the Devil was attacking God's Elect. While most remain unknown except through the record of their names in the witchcraft trial papers, some are more noteworthy due to their own activities. One such was a minster of Coldingham, Christopher Knowles. It was Knowles who was minister at Coldingham when Sir Alexander Home's father had 'caused to burn seven or eight of them.' He was involved in three cases in 1629: that of Helen Huldie, Marion Sandersoun and Margaret Loche.[89] He was involved in several more cases throughout the 1630s in which John Home sat as a Commissioner. However, in 1641, he was dismissed from his post for the crime of adultery. Knowles was originally from Swynewood and was ordained as a minister in 1616 and found a post in Spott under the patronage of Sir Alexander Home the elder, father of Sir Patrick. In 1622, he moved to take up the ministry at Coldingham.[90] When the accusation of adultery was laid against Knowles, he was defended by Sir John Home but he was found guilty and dismissed from the Kirk and turned out of his living. The accusation that resulted in his dismissal had not, however, been the first charge laid against him and it is possible that he could have been dismissed earlier had it not been for the support of the Home family. Given these challenges, it is likely that Knowles would have been extremely zealous in his duty to root out witches, possibly even to the extent of turning a blind eye to any irregularities at the very least.

Black's Calendar lists several instances of witch false imprisonments, broddings and 'executions' that took place without the benefit of a trial. In 1630, Catie Wilson of Stow was to be 'tried by jobbing (brodding)'; no Commission record.[91] In 1650, a man Waddell was 'burnt'; no trial record.[92] In 1675, an old woman and her daughter, Helen Stewart, were burned for witchcraft; no trial record.[93] In 1678, in Loanhead, 'nine or ten women burnt for witchcraft'; no trial record.[94] In 1705, Janet Corphat was murdered by 'the rabble.[95] Of course, in some of these cases, the trial records may have gone missing over the years but it is clear at least in some of the cases, eg Janet Corphat, that no trial took place.

Given the ongoing disruption of the results of the Reformation, the effects of plague, famine and war and the added pressures of an old area of worship, a coastal location and a minister that had a reputation to redeem, it is no wonder that Coldingham succumbed to the worst excesses of the witchcraft frenzy and became the site of at least one illegal execution.

14

Selkirk, 1700

'the drier ye are, the better ye'll burn'

AS THE CENTURY started to draw to a close, the number of witch trials and executions started to reduce. Commissioners and lawyers became aware of the number of confessions that were being retracted and gradually became less than convinced of the rigour of some of the proofs being offered in many trials. Possible miscarriages of justice, which had increased as the number of trials had increased, worried some as they feared they could undermine the legal system as a whole. This was compounded by the cases of several witch brodders who were found to be frauds. Brodding for the Devil's mark was no longer used as evidence of witchcraft. Communities were increasingly wary of paying for a service that did not deliver results. Confession under torture also fell from favour due to the large number of retractions that had occurred. Challenges from some of those accused of witchcraft had also raised concerns. If a man, or a wealthy well-connected woman, could successfully challenge their accusers such that the accusation was withdrawn, what did that mean for the whole system? Procedures in the interrogation and investigation of suspected witches had been tightened over the century but abuses still occurred and innocents were still burned in marketplaces and town squares.

What was not in doubt, however, was that witches and witchcraft existed. This view, being held more persistently in Scotland than most other European countries, remained steadfast. The problem was not whether or not witches existed or that they committed the crime of witchcraft, everyone knew and believed both to be true. Rather, the problem was how to prove it. The world was changing and the debates and disputes on witchcraft and how to deal with it were also evolving. Most arguments revolved round how to prove witchcraft within an increasingly sophisticated legal system and some even questioned whether this was a matter for the courts at all but was better left to church authorities.

A few voices were also starting to question the existence of witches at all. European philosophers discussed the phenomenon of witchcraft and its manifestations. Cases in which witches had recanted their confessions interested the philosophers. What was the nature of truth and reality? Were these beliefs in supernatural power and a pact with the Devil imaginary or a temporary delusion? The old arguments about the weak and inferior nature of women contributed to these arguments. Would the Devil really be interested in women or was this not a case of foolish women fantasising about sex? The confessions of accused witches were the delusions of inferior women who possibly thought the meetings and sexual congress to be real at the time but when faced with the reality of execution the delusion dissolved away. Why, if the courts in most cases refused to allow women to speak, were they listening to this nonsense? If Auld Nick was really stalking the land, why did he use these inferior beings to attack men? And was he truly abroad anyway? The worst excesses of the 17th century were fading away. The four horsemen of the Apocalypse that had seemed to ride across Europe in the first half of the century were now no longer to be seen. The Thirty Years' War was over. The Peace of Westphalia had been signed. Britain had rejected republicanism and restored its King. Initially these discussions were confined to a few philosophical types in the universities. But few though they were, they were influential and their numbers grew, causing others to have doubts. Alarmed by this apparent lapse of faith, churches throughout Europe, both Protestant and Catholic, recognised that to counter such blasphemous ideas, witchcraft trials needed to be beyond reproach.

In Scotland, the twin attacks of legal rigour and philosophical inquiry induced the authorities to ensure the rigour of the case brought against a witch could not be in doubt. Reform was needed. The Scottish Kirk combined, therefore, with the legal establishment to tighten the trial procedures to ensure competent verdicts for both spiritual and temporal reasons.

This process started in 1661–2 after the great witch hunt of that period which had involved over 660 individuals over four Scottish counties. The trials had been so numerous and the death toll so large that several abuses had taken place. Moreover, these abuses had been obvious to all. These abuses included the unauthorised arrest of suspects, the use of torture without a warrant to carry out the same, brodding suspects without a warrant and the use of walking and watching suspects who were illegally held. Guilty verdicts had been reached and executions had been rapidly carried out but not without disquiet being voiced by many. The apparent zeal of the Kirk to secure convictions was seen, by some, as an opportunity for the local ministers and elders to get rid of some troublemakers while terrorising others. After these abuses, and the public criticisms they raised, there was a gradual change in how cases were conducted. The authorities started to take more control over cases, the use of torture and brodding was reduced and a more stringent use of evidence as proof was initiated. This legal control also chimed with a new mood in the political atmosphere in Scotland. Members of the nobility who were neither churchmen or lawyers had started to flex their political muscles. The return of King Charles II in 1660 had made many in Scotland pause and consider who held authority in the land. Many felt that the Kirk had for too long held sway over matters that should not concern them. Ministers and Kirk elders could chase witches all they liked but they could not and should not hold authority over the local nobility. The minister's role in directing the local nobility who sat as Commissioners in witchcraft trials was under threat.

The courts, conscious of what they could and could not prove, opted for a new act that repealed the 1563 Act but outlawed any person who 'pretend to exercise or use any kind of Witchcraft, Sorcery, Inchantment, or Conjuration, or undertake to tell Fortunes, or pretend, from his or her Skill or Knowledge in any occult or crafty Science, foretune telling'.[96] By repealing the 1563 Act, in theory witchcraft was no longer illegal. It was a neat trick. The Act relegated witches and witchcraft to the margins of society and released the courts from having to deal with the matter without denying their existence. The detection and punishment of witches and witchcraft were now solely under the jurisdiction of the Kirk.

During the 17th century, most witchcraft trials in the Borders were local trials. The local clergy rarely sent their witches to

Edinburgh for trial and only ever bothered with the authorities in
Edinburgh to get the most basic necessary legal permissions. This,
however, proved to be their very undoing. Obtaining a Commission
to try witches, locals then went ahead to arrest, investigate, interrogate and try witches. In their enthusiasm to bring the guilty to
trial, warrants were not always obtained for those other than the
main suspect. Torture was often used without formal permission,
to excess or on those underage or mentally unstable. In some cases,
those found not guilty or not proven were not released as they
should have been but continued to be held while the Kirk minister
and elders sought for additional proof. In some instances, the trial
was simply held again with the same evidence presented to the same
jury. This was particularly true of those found not proven. There
are no cases noted where a second not guilty or not proven verdict
was returned.

As the central authorities started to take a greater interest in the
trials, these irregularities came to light. As the laxity of some of the
Borders trials became known, the authorities insisted on a greater
degree of compliance with the correct procedures. Privy Councillors,
anxious to distance themselves from anything that might damage
their reputation, laid the blame squarely at the feet of the Kirk. Local
Commissioners kept their heads down as their loyalties became
divided. True Borderers they might have been but they could see
the way the wind was blowing. The political mood was changing,
albeit slowly and ambition often won out over local loyalty. As the
century entered its final quarter the zeal of witch hunting among
the local nobility was replaced with a desire to consolidate local
power against the authorities in Edinburgh. Commissioners still sat
on trials but were quite happy for any criticisms to fall on the Kirk.
Borders' Commissioners would still sign an order for torture to be
used but would make note that the request had come from the local
Kirk minister.

The issue of torture was a thorny one for the courts. Torture
was a perfectly acceptable method by which to obtain confessions
in many cases of witchcraft, and in several other crimes. The problem was the use of torture without permission. In 1662, the Privy
Council noted that many innocent persons had been executed as a
result of confessions obtained under torture; these persons having

retracted their confessions just before being executed. As some of those put to torture were young or ill, the courts felt these confessions to be unsafe, although not necessarily untrue. The individuals might be guilty but retracted confessions were always an embarrassment to the legal system as was the use of torture on children and those addled in their wits. And while most of the accused were thought to have probably been guilty, some might indeed have been innocent. The Kirk, however, took a different view. Retraction, in the minds of almost all ministers and elders, was simply further proof of the wickedness of the Devil and the perfidiousness of witches. It inflamed the crowds with false notions and was the reason why accused witches should not be allowed to speak before being executed. Some members of the Kirk thought to challenge the law and demand that those convicted of the 'foul cryme of witchcraft' be denied the opportunity to speak. However, as the guilty had to be asked, before their execution, if they publicly renounced their sins and asked God for his forgiveness, it was impossible to deny them the chance to speak.

As a result of these dubious executions, after 1662, torture was made illegal unless specific permission was granted by the Privy Council. Any minister applying for permission to use torture had first to show cause why it was necessary. If granted, torture was to be used with the utmost care. It was to be used sparingly to produce confessions from those already named as witches, not as a first resort by local authorities. While there is abundant evidence of its continuing illegal use in the Borders as late as 1698, its overall use did decrease. Permissions for the use of torture became harder to obtain as just cause for its use had to be shown. As a result, confessions became more difficult to obtain leading to higher rates of acquittals.

As the century wound on, there was also an increased desire to test the evidence brought before the courts. Scottish courts did allow witches a defence of sorts, although few could afford the fees of an advocate and the Kirk challenged the accused's right under the provisions of the Poor Roll. Nevertheless, advocates, when present, started to question the proofs brought against suspected witches. Was an ill child really bewitched or was it not more likely that the child was sick from natural causes? Witnesses were questioned not only about what they saw but as to their motives. How truthful were they in their testimony? This was a turning point for many. Many advocates relished the thought of testing out their oratorical abilities in witchcraft trials where such questions could be examined. As normal criminal cases gave no such opportunity, some ambitious advocates would take on witchcraft trials simply in order to make a name for themselves.

However, in many local trials in the Borders, the problem was not who could afford to pay for an advocate but where could an advocate be found who was willing to take the case. Making a name for yourself in the Borders was a very different matter. The close-knit nature of the area meant that advocates, just as in the case of the Commissioners, might well be related to and would definitely be well known by the local minister who was in charge of the investigation. Advocates who asked awkward questions during a trial had to live in the same community after the case was over. And while rigour of evidence might hold sway in Edinburgh, the Kirk was master in the Borders. Faced with the difficult choice of challenging the local Kirk establishment by taking on a suspected witch as a client and with the still prevalent view that witches existed few advocates stepped forward. Again, the Borders held out longer than most regions but eventually advocates from Edinburgh and the Lothians came down to local trials and the central authorities moved greater numbers of trials to Edinburgh. Border advocates, keen not to be seen as behind the times in their legal practice and not wishing to lose clients to Edinburgh lawyers, also began to question witnesses. The momentum built up such that challenging evidence that had previously been accepted without question became *de rigueur* and acquittals rates started to rise.

It must be remembered, however, that it was not the central authorities or advocates that decided the guilt or innocence of a witch. That remained with the jury of local individuals. Jury selection was on the grounds of good character and good character was still decided by the local Kirk session. The prosecuting minister therefore had an inbuilt bias in the jury. All the legal procedures in the land and all the fancy advocates from Edinburgh could not, in many cases, influence a jury to find a suspect innocent. A jury's logic, if cruel in its consequences, was as least consistent.

Everyone knew witchcraft existed. The minister suspected witch-craft. The minister had a suspect arrested. The minister interro-gated the suspect. The minister produced evidence that showed the suspect's guilt, including a confession. Therefore, the suspect was guilty. If the defence advocates were to be believed, then the witch was innocent and the minister must have been wrong. Indeed, the amount of involvement that the local minister had in witchcraft trials meant that the innocence of a witch implied that the minster was more than wrong but was a liar. For a long time that was a step too far for many juries in rural Borders. However, as more and more trials were carried out with more and more evidence being challenged, the weight of opinion from advocates and judges tipped the balance in favour of the law and the Kirk lost out.

With a refusal to allow torture, a reduction in confessions and an increase in advocates questioning evidence, the witchcraft trials were becoming meaningless. The belief in witchcraft remained as strong as ever, especially among the Kirk, but the courts were no longer the place in which to punish the guilty.

As in all matters that emanate from the centre, it often takes time to percolate to rural areas and the conduct of witchcraft trials in the Borders was no exception. The local clergy were well aware of the continuing and steadfast belief in witchcraft prevalent in Scottish society and while the judiciary might trouble themselves over legal niceties, the Borders clergy continued as before encour-aging a robust level of investigation and interrogation. While the argument over proving the gainsayers wrong in the matter of the existence of witches occupied the higher echelons of the Kirk, on the ground local presbyteries stubbornly retained their own meth-ods of interrogation often with the tacit approval of the Kirk hier-archy. On this occasion, however, they were on the losing side and the judiciary, with their insistence on rigorous evidential based tri-als, won out and in 1736 had the law changed.

The end of witchcraft trials did not, however, mean an end to witchcraft accusations or executions. Abandoned, as they felt, by the judiciary, local communities were left to find their own solutions to the problems of witches in their midst. In the Borders, as in some other areas of Scotland, the local solution was simple. Lynch the witches. Illness and harvest failure still occurred, accusations were still made and Kirk ministers investigated. Suspects were rounded up and torture was applied. But no trial took place. Convinced of the suspect's guilt, local communities then worriet, burned, hanged, drowned and stoned to death the accused. No records exist of any arrests made in the Borders for these murders. Kirk involvement varied from parish to parish. Some ministers became conveniently deaf and blind to the local mob that dragged women from their houses and drowned them in the river, some openly collaborated with their local communities taking part in the interrogation of suspects; still others used their pulpits to exhort their flock 'thou shalt not suffer a witch to live'.

In 1700, the last recorded witch execution took place in the Scottish Borders in Selkirk. Meg Lawson, a local woman, was tried, found guilty and executed of the crime of 'foul wytchcraft'.[97] The tide had been turning against the trials for some time but came too late for Meg. She was executed before a large and noisy crowd who were, as one visiting minister remarked, 'showing great drunkenness and were much given to abusing all around including the clergy'.[98] Meg was to prove a great afternoon's entertainment for them.

Selkirk in 1700 was becoming a thriving merchant town. The past century had seen turbulent times with the battle of Philiphaugh still a raw memory for many in the town. However, there had also been the incorporation of many of the town's craft guilds and it seemed that the violent old days were behind Selkirk. The new century loomed promising trade and wealth as the town looked to markets both north and south. But for every new merchant's house, there were equally back wynds with low mean cottages. And below the confident air of the new times, old superstitions still ran deep.

Selkirk had seen its fair share of witchcraft trials throughout the century with as many as 20 having faced the rope and the flame. Determined as any Border town to drive out Auld Nick, changes in legal procedures handed down from Edinburgh were viewed with a mixture of suspicion and disrespect. Selkirk felt itself quite capable of dealing with its own without interference from the central authorities. The relationship with Edinburgh was tainted with an old memory. In the 14th century when the Black Death had visited Scotland, the authorities in Edinburgh had closed the border with England, the border being fixed at the mid-point of the river Tweed.

Unfortunately, Selkirk's position to the south of the river caused it to be cut off from the rest of Scotland and, of course, from England. Stranded in no-man's land, it had taken several weeks and bags of coin to get the authorities to admit and rectify their mistake. In the meantime, the people of Selkirk who had not succumbed to the plague had almost died of starvation as supplies to the town had been blocked. Any edicts that were sent down to Selkirk from Edinburgh were, therefore, frequently ignored.

Meg Lawson was a familiar figure round the town. Known as a healer, she was frequently consulted over childbirth and in cases of sickness. As ever, this could prove to be a dangerous profession and for Meg more so than most, as she also had a certain reputation. Meg was a convicted witch.

First arrested and tried in 1662 after an accusation of witchcraft, Meg had quickly confessed to being a witch and was found guilty.[99] For some reason, she had escaped the flames that time. Had her offence been relatively mild? Had she shown remorse and promised to return to the Kirk? Whatever had happened, she had served her punishment and then returned to her life in the town. The locals in Selkirk seem to have accepted her back without too much resentment and she was soon being sought by those in need of her cures and charms. In 1700, however, she was rearrested. The charges were familiar – illness of a child – but then a startling accusation of metamorphosis was laid. Meg, it seemed, had the power to turn herself into a mouse. And it was as that mouse that she had apparently crept into people's homes to lay sickness on their children. This seems far-fetched. Invited into homes to help with childbirth or to heal a sick bairn, Meg had ample opportunity to cast her spells. What need had she to change into a mouse? And yet the accusation remained. Was the Kirk worried that she might not be found guilty? Meg was tried alone, not as part of a larger scare in the community. She was a single, elderly, poor woman, relatively well liked, or at least tolerated, about the town and as such was no threat to anyone. So was this a genuine case of witchcraft or was the Kirk tidying up from a previous error? Was the mouse story added to ensure a guilty verdict? Metamorphosis accusations were not unknown in Scotland but were certainly very rare and almost always resulted in a guilty verdict as they were considered proof of real occult power.

Poor Meg with her precarious existence was hardly the epitome of a powerful witch but whatever the truth of the matter, mouse or no mouse, she was found guilty again and this time would face the flames.

The great time of burnings was drawing to a close and Meg's guilt appeared no more solid that the last time, so what had changed? True, this was a second offence. And the Kirk, possibly embarrassed that they had not secured an execution in the previous trial, had not changed in its attitude. But one thing had changed and that was Meg herself. No longer remorseful, possibly, but no longer young, definitely. An old woman, on her own, accused of laying sickness on a child, she was unfortunate in that she fitted the Kirk's stereotype of the old witch perfectly. The old ways were indeed drawing to a close and the Kirk knew it but they would go out in the Borders with a flourish supplied by old Meg Lawson.

After the guilty verdict and the sentence of death, Meg was confined to a cell in the tolbooth where she awaited execution. She did not have to wait long. Three days after the trial, she rose for the last time. Dressed in a thin hair shift, bare foot and bare headed and with her hands bound behind her back by the baillie, Meg was prepared for her execution.

However, for some reason there was a delay. The crowd outside the tolbooth waited for Meg and, as they waited, passed the time in the town's various ale shops. They were getting restless by the time she finally appeared. Accompanied by the baillie's men, she was led up the Kirk Wynd accompanied by the prayers of the minister that were almost drowned out by the shouts and comments of the crowd.

At the foot of the Foul Brig Port, Meg stumbled and begged for a drink from the fetid pool that gave the brig its name. 'Na, na na,' said the hangman. 'The drier ye are, the better ye'll burn.'[100] At this piece of wit a great cheer went up from the crowd. Pulled to her feet, Meg was dragged up to the top of Gallows Knowe. The minister, puffing slightly, arrived and exhorted her, at this her final hour, to accept her fate and consign her soul to God. The crowd leaned forward and fell silent, eager for some more spectacle and Meg did not disappoint. She raised her head and with her hair wild about her, she muttered something under her breath, too soft for the crowd to hear yet loud enough and wicked enough for the minister to blanch and take a step back. An excited thrill went through the crowd. The minister recovered himself and nodded to the baillie. Two men stepped forward and held Meg's arms as the executioner quickly slipped the noose around her neck and placed a small piece of wood under the rope. He then twisted the piece of wood quickly to strangle Meg. A quiet gurgling could be heard but didn't last long, Meg was an old woman on the margins of life and there wasn't much fight left in her old body. She quickly slipped away. Her lifeless body was dragged to the pyre and a couple of strokes of the tar brush applied to the hair shift before the fire was solemnly lit. The minister started his sermon. A sudden breeze caught the flames and the fire roared to life, echoed by a great cheer from the crowd. The minister started again to be met by more abuse and a flying neep that just missed his ear. Glaring at his disreputable flock, he gave up on the soul of Meg Lawson and turned tail. It was alleged that he had spent that evening writing to the presbytery asking to transfer to another parish, even one in Glasgow.

Conclusion

BETWEEN 1600 AND 1700, almost every area in Scotland was awash with witch trials; but what drove the accusations and trials of so many witches in the Borders was a result of the combination of a particular set of circumstances.

The Borders was a land of rural communities, worn down by the fragility of a poor rural existence and with a recent history of reivers in the night. They also suffered the ravages of recent and, no doubt to them, seemingly unending warfare. They had endured repeated cycles of plague and famine. The world had become a confusing and frightening place over which the individual had little or no control. The innocent fell ill alongside the wicked; the pious and ungodly were equally afflicted; hard work and thriftiness were no guarantee against starvation. These stresses would have been articulated and thus relieved by accusations of witchcraft. Someone had to be to blame. Those who were known to have 'powers' and who had previously used charms to heal a sick child or 'blessed' a new cow to give good milk were now suspect. The accusations and activities that would have been firmly dealt with in previous times with harsh condemnation, excommunication and some form of punishment were now ruthlessly pursued to the furthest extent of the law by Kirk elders in the Borders. Witchcraft was no longer seen as a misguided activity but as a diabolical evil.

Witchcraft was a real and genuine fear in Scotland in the late 16th and early 17th centuries and should not just be dismissed as the foolishness of ill-educated common people. Belief in the spirit world and supernatural power in a time before modern medicine and rational belief helped to make sense of an often cruel and harsh existence. The Devil and his minions were real entities that could, and did, wreak havoc in individual's lives. The faeries folk were equally real and could, on occasions, be induced to help. But what had been around for several hundred years as a relatively harmless belief system with many positive benefits, at least where the faeries were concerned, became a victim of a particular set of circumstances. War, famine, disease and religious upheaval all combined to turn belief in the power of witchcraft to a fear of witches. It is difficult for the modern mind to conceive of the ease with which fear of witches could consume a community. What is worth recalling is the role of the Kirk in the Borders in taking that fear and turning it into hysteria. Like the Kirk elsewhere, the Borders' clergy perceived themselves to be under attack because of their very godliness. In addition, they felt a genuine sense of fear about the threat, as they saw it, of the Catholic in the north of England providing a source of and sanctuary for witches. They had also to deal with their lack of involvement with the Covenanters. They, the self-proclaimed God's Elect, had failed to rally to the cause. However, that guilt and shame might be somewhat assuaged if the Kirk was involved in other, equally important work for the Lord: combating witches. Frightened by Catholics, shamed by Covenanters and attempting to deal with the apparent chaos all around them, the response of the Borders Kirk was to unleash a wave of torture and ill treatment that would consume every village and town in the Borders and cost at least 245 people their lives.

In 1736, the Scottish Witchcraft Act was formally repealed by Parliament. It was replaced by the Witchcraft Act of the British Isles. Ostensibly decriminalising witchcraft, the new act relegated witches to the jurisdiction of the churches. It also demanded a much higher emphasis on real evidence and introduced a more rigorous approach to proofs in criminal trials. Confession, so important previously but so open to abuse under interrogation, would no longer be considered as absolute proof. The modern world was dawning with a greater understanding of and faith in science and hard fact. The age of superstition was slipping away.

While many in the Kirk were aware of the danger of abuses where witchcraft trials were undertaken, their belief in witchcraft remained unshaken. While they might support the introduction of some form of rigour in the case of evidence, many privately still held on to the belief in confession as proof positive. They, after all, lived in the real world of towns and villages where crops still failed and babies still died for unknown reasons that the new sciences could still not explain. In 1773, amid the flowering of the Scottish Enlightenment, the divines of the Associated Presbytery of Scotland passed a resolution affirming their belief in witchcraft.

In 1830, Sir Walter Scott's *Letters on Demonology and Witchcraft* was published. The *Letters* is a wide-ranging thesis on supernatural beliefs and tales including much besides witchcraft. Scott was able to draw on many local anecdotes for the book despite its basic premise being that no one believed in such nonsense anymore. The Enlightenment had apparently done its work and superstitious beliefs had been banished to the history books, lingering on only in folk memories and a few local customs. But perhaps there was more than just memory to be discovered. Letter nine contains several stories of witchcraft beliefs and trials but finishes with a curious tale. This anecdote tells of a farmer who out walking one day met a woman who cursed him with such vehemence he felt it necessary to go the Sheriff. When the Sheriff approached the woman, she, far from denying the act, was quite as ease with the powers that she had. All three, the farmer, the woman and the Sheriff found the existence of such supernatural powers perfectly normal. The story, which Scott claimed was true, had taken place in the Scottish Borders at the turn of the new century, 1800.

Appendix A
The cultural background
of the witchcraft trials

THIS APPENDIX GIVES further information about ten aspects of the cultural background to the witchcraft trials. This includes ideas around mental illness; beliefs that remain prevalent today; the roots of Halloween; information about the men who sat in judgement of supposed witches; how some of this justice was dispensed; the religious justification for that justice; and finally the backdrop of plague, the reivers and the role of witches as healers.

1 Addled in their wits

In the 17th century, both Scottish doctors and the law recognised two main forms of mental illness: madness, which was a general term for all mental illness, and those who were addled in their wits, which included those who had 'grown feeble due to age' or those considered 'simple' from birth. Under the law, those who were mad or addled in their wits could not be held legally responsible for their actions and they could not be used as witnesses in a trial. Those who were addled in their wits were usually cared for by their families. For those classed as mad, unfit to look after themselves or dangerous to others, there were the correction houses. These houses were found in larger cities such as Glasgow or Edinburgh and varied in the care they offered; most gave their inmates basic food, clothing and bedding but little else. Treatment was non-existent for most as most forms of madness were thought to be incurable. Individuals who were known to harm themselves were frequently restrained in chains.

In many witchcraft trials, care was taken that suspects and witnesses were of sound mind to ensure that the law was not brought

into disrepute. Although the belief in witchcraft was considered
normal, it was recognised that the mad could be deluded into
thinking they had powers and had met the Devil. However, it was
also accepted that an individual could be mentally ill and a witch.
In some instances, madness was thought to have been brought on
by contact with Auld Nick and was thus considered a just punishment. Many, however, believed madness to be feigned and just
another trick inspired by the Devil. Those thought to be pretending
to be mad were frequently beaten or doused with cold water to try
to break them of their 'wicked pretence'. Those who were addled
in their wits presented a further problem. If they were truly addled
then surely the Devil would not use them? Or would he, the great
trickster, use those that would not be suspected? Had they been
addled by contact with him? Or were they deluding themselves? Or
were they, like those that were mad, feigning?

Few, if any trials, consulted doctors about the state of mind of
the accused and within this confusion of beliefs, the interpretation
of the law rarely protected any but the most severely delusional.

2 Belief in witchcraft

Belief in witchcraft is often denigrated as a peculiarity of our superstitious and ignorant ancestors. However, in 21st century Scotland
there are still some who believe that:

- a black cat crossing your path is unlucky – a black cat was
  a witch's familiar (a creature thought to share the witch's
  supernatural power)
- a Rowan tree is lucky – Rowan trees were thought to ward
  off witches
- throwing a penny down a wishing well is lucky – pagan
  Scots made votive offerings of metal, which was precious,
  into a body of water to appease the gods (water was considered a gateway to the gods)
- spilt salt should be thrown over the left shoulder to prevent
  bad luck – the salt will stop the Devil seeing you
- white heather is lucky – white heather is very rare and only
  grows where faeries stop to rest and so is touched with
  faerie magic and luck

- a horseshoe brings good luck – but must be the right way up or Auld Nick will pull the luck out
- seeing one magpie is unlucky – a single magpie seen near the window of a house is a sign of impending death, because magpies carry a drop of the Devil's blood on their tongues
- touching wood brings good luck – the cross was made of wood and repels the Devil
- the empty shell from a boiled egg should always be pierced to let the Devil out
- a ring with a pearl is unlucky – pearls symbolise tears and will bring sadness
- the tooth fairy will leave money under our pillows in exchange for our teeth – the first tooth that a child lost was to be carefully rolled up in a sheet of paper lined with salt and hidden in a hole made by a mouse to bring strong healthy teeth
- the groom must carry the bride over the threshold – to stop Auld Nick nipping at her ankles
- the number 13 is unlucky – Christ with his 12 disciples made a group of 13; Judas, as the betrayer of Christ, was considered the 13th man

3 Halloween

Halloween originated in the Celtic festival of Samhain. Regarded as the Celtic New Year, it was a celebration of the end of harvest and a time of plenty. A good harvest meant that the community had sufficient food to survive through the winter. But it was also the time when the boundaries between the world of the living and the world of the dead faded away, allowing the dead to pass from their realm to the world of the living. It was the time of the year when the living honoured the dead and paid their respects to departed family members. Tales were told of the heroism and battles that the departed had undertaken and won, the forerunner of today's ghost stories.

All of the fires in the locality were extinguished and a single new fire created or 'forced' in the centre of the village and this became the 'need fire' from which each household then lit their new fire for the year. A great feast would be prepared which involved the slaughter of large numbers of livestock and their bones would be thrown onto the 'need fire' which then became the bone-fire (bon-fire). A single firebrand would be carried sunwise around the village and the surrounding fields to protect them over the coming winter. The meat of the slaughtered livestock would be salted and then eaten over the coming winter. Autumn foods such as apples and nuts would be eaten and also used for divination about what the winter might bring. Apples were plucked from moving water (bobbing for apples) and nuts were roasted to see which way they moved.

The spirits that returned from the dead were often thought to have special knowledge, which, if asked by the right people, they might share with the living. Certain members of society were thought able to talk to the dead spirits and were held in high status. The Christian church was particularly harsh on necromancy and accusations of talking to the dead were frequently levelled at many in witchcraft trials. However, not all the spirits that returned were friendly. Some were merely lonely for their living relatives and would try to take the living back to the land of the dead with them for company. Others were more malevolent, possibly the restless spirits of evildoers out for mischief among the living. In order to hide from these spirits, faces would be blacked and disguises worn to hide from spirits and songs sung to placate the dead, the origins of guising in Scotland today.

4 The rise of the guid men

Scottish society was divided into three rough groupings in the 17th century: the aristocracy, the middling ranks and the poor. The aristocracy comprised the dukes, earls, viscounts, parliamentary lords and the lairds. The middling ranks was a broad group of ten-ant farmers, merchants and artisans and guild masters. The poor were mostly farm labourers, town workers and the destitute. The church had originally sat alongside such groupings with cardinals coming from aristocratic families, bishops living and working with merchants and some parish priests barely more literate than their parishioners. In some cases, the priests would conduct services by reciting the mass in Latin which they had merely memorised with little understanding of the true meaning of the words.

By the time of the Reformation, the three groupings remained in place but the creation of the Protestant Kirk had wrought two main changes. Firstly, everyone in the newly formed Kirk had to be literate. Ministers were to lead their congregation into an understanding of scripture, not to bamboozle them with meaningless ritual. The Kirk was supported in this by the lairds, the lowest members of the Scottish aristocracy. As a result, after the departure of James VI and his court to London, the authority of the Kirk rose. This in turn helped to consolidate the power of the local lairds, the guid men. The ability and willingness of the lairds to dispense justice in local areas suited the higher aristocracy that sat on the Privy Council.

5 Jethart justice – 'first hang a man syne judge him'

Justice in 17th Scotland could be and frequently was both swift and brutal. In 1603, when King James VI of Scotland succeeded to the English throne, one of his first acts was to subdue the wild Border lands of the reivers. James was determined to prove himself a modern monarch, the equal of any in Europe and used the subjugation of the Borders as proof of this. How could he present himself as the ruler of a civilised land if his southern border was populated by wild men that refused to recognise the rule of law? He appointed new men to oversee Borders' justice by means of a purge of the most troublesome families. Deeply resented by the reiving families as interference in their way of life, the arrival of a centralised legal authority in the Borders was fiercely resisted by many. Other reiver families realised which way the wind was starting to blow, quickly put away their reiving ways and declared their loyalty to the King. As they knew both the terrain and those reivers who refused to comply with the new laws, the newly loyal ex-reiving families were frequently appointed as the new authorities in control. As such, these ex-reivers knew who to hang and where to find them and frequently dispensed with the formality of a trial merely executing known felons. Conveniently, in some cases, these known felons happened to be men from rival families whose land fell forfeit. Jedburgh was to see mass hangings that ripped the heart out of many families and gave birth to the legend of Jethart Justice, where it was said the authorities dealing with the reivers 'first hang a man syne judge him'.

The reality, however, was somewhat different. 17th century justice was indeed swift and brutal but it was also based on the law. When James VI decided to deal with the troublesome border lands, he did so by appointing Lords of the Marches to investigate the reivers and bring them to account for their actions. The folk of the Borders were only too eager to swear out complaints against the reivers and while some, no doubt, were merely a continuation of the various feuds between reiver families most were genuine complaints of reiver attacks. Far from romantic figures brutally suppressed by tyranny, most reivers were cattle thieves, murderers and rapists. Most were well known to the authorities and while some of the authorities in Jedburgh may have been over-zealous in their execution of the law and hanged known reivers before trying them, most were arrested, tried and convicted through the courts before being punished. By 1610, the hangings were over as many reiving families had fled, been deported or died at the end of a rope.[101]

The speed with which the reivers, after so many years, were suppressed, the numbers executed and deported and the cases of execution without trial that did in fact take place, left many families in the Borders without a male head of the house and destroyed a way of life. Many families had to come to terms with the psychological shock of this sudden change. The reality of having been part of a brutal and violent way of life may have been too painful to acknowledge for some. The legend of Jethart Justice and the romanticisation of the reivers may have been an easier method of coping with their changed circumstances.

Despite the bloody and violent reputation of the reivers, the Local Authority of the Scottish Borders currently uses the logo of a reiver on horseback as part of its corporate branding.

6 Kramer[102]

Heinrich Kramer was born around 1430 in Schlettstadt, Alsace on the border of modern-day Germany and France. He trained for the church and gained a reputation as an impressive lecturer in theology. Known for his passionate beliefs, he served time in gaol for defamatory remarks he made during a sermon about the Holy Roman Emperor Frederick III. After his release, he was made Dominican inquisitor for the province of Teutonia. Around 1460, he went to Rome to continue his studies. His time there was marred with at least one street brawl in which he was probably the instigator. No charges were levelled against him although he became a 'person of note' for the authorities. On his return to Schlettstadt, he became involved in a conflict with a local priest and was arrested on the orders of Pope Sixtus IV for theft and he lost his position. He managed to redeem himself and regained his position as inquisitor. He spent the next few years travelling and investigating cases of heresy and witchcraft. In 1485, he arrived in Innsbruck, becoming involved in the witchcraft trial of 50 women. Kramer believed witchcraft was a reality; the local bishop, Georg Golser, however, thought witchcraft was an illusion caused by evil spirits. These different beliefs were to prove insurmountable. Kramer investigated the allegations against the women thoroughly, including using torture and close questioning about the sexual behaviour of the women. Golser objected to Kramer's methods and appointed an overseer for the trials who was more disposed to the bishop's views. When the trial started, Kramer's investigations and the evidence resulting from them were ruled inadmissible. All of the women were acquitted. Kramer was both humiliated and angry and had to leave Innsbruck under threat of violence from the women's families. In 1486, he wrote the *Malleus Maleficarum*. The book was intended to instruct legal authorities how to prosecute witches. As witchcraft was, by its very nature, a largely unseen crime and as witches with the help of the Devil were both tricky and deceitful, prosecuting them was fraught with difficulties as the trial at Innsbruck had shown. The *Malleus* was Kramer's attempt to help others with this tricky problem as well as a defence of his own beliefs and attempt to repair the damage done to his reputation during the Innsbruck trial.

The book is long and complex dealing not only with witches and how to identify and prosecute them but, no doubt as a rebuke to Bishop Golser, also discusses those who lack the mettle to pursue witches with extreme and steadfast purpose. Kramer tried to obtain endorsement for the *Malleus* from the Inquisition of the University of Cologne, but far from recommending the work the university theologians considered it unethical, promoted illegal procedures and inconsistent with Catholic doctrines on demonology. Controversial to the last, Kramer forged a letter of recommendation about the *Malleus* from the university which resulted in another court case against him. In his later years, he withdrew from witchcraft trials and spent his time writing manuscripts on theology. He died in 1505.

The *Malleus Maleficarum* remained the standard reference book on witchcraft for many years and, despite being written by a Catholic, would continue to be so even after the Reformation in both Protestant and Catholic countries alike.

7 Plague

Plague was an all too common occurrence in the 17th century and the fact of its frequency, and the confusion over exactly what it was, did little to lessen the fear and panic its very name could instil in a population.

In 1349, the Scots and the English were once again indulging in their respective national pastimes of fighting each other in the Scottish Borders. The Scots were attempting to rescue their young King, David II, who was languishing in the luxury of Windsor castle since his capture in 1346. Gathered in Selkirk forest, the Scots fervently believed that God was on their side and this was 'proved' when reports were received that the English army had started to sicken and die of an unknown and foul disease. This was surely God's punishment on the English for their wicked ways. Unfortunately, the 'foul death of the English' was no respecter of geographical boundaries or nationality and, when the Scots charged over the border and down into Northumbria, it was only a matter of time before they too succumbed. The Scots army fled in disarray before the pestilence and carried the disease to their homes and families throughout Scotland.

The plague that had felled the English, and then the Scots, was the Great Pestilence that had arrived in Great Weymouth in the spring of 1349 and travelled up the length of England until it reached Northumbria and the English and Scots armies.

The Great Pestilence (the term the Black Death was invented around 1800) devastated Europe, killing around 20 million, about a third of the population at the time, and changing life for ever.

It has been credited with ushering in the end of the feudal system in some countries and so marked society that the folk memory of the ensuing horror lingered on for several centuries. What struck terror into the hearts of many communities was the speed of spread and the apparent indiscriminate manner in which some individuals lived while others died writhing in agony as the black buboes or swellings attacked the victims. In Scotland, Hector Boece, the great chronicler wrote,

> Sic pestilence rang ouir all Scotland
> Richt venomous, quilk smyttit hes so smart
> Of the pepill deuorit the third part[103]

Two hundred and fifty years later, the start of the new century was marked by outbreaks of plague – had the Great Pestilence returned?

Of the six outbreaks of plague that were seen in the Borders in the 17th century, none was the return of the Great Pestilence. Cholera or Typhoid are the most likely culprits. This was, however, no comfort to those in villages and towns when the cry went up – plague. What would it be this time – Cholera, Typhoid? Both resulted in death. Was it even the return of the Great Pestilence? London, that great city of sin and iniquity, had seen the Great Pestilence return in 1666 when around 100,000 died.

Plague, in all its forms, was surely sent by God as a punishment for the sins of the wicked but, as had been seen in the Great Pestilence, had also inexplicably killed the Godly. With such an unknowable and deadly foe, fear of the plague, in whatever form and within the political chaos of the 17th century, was entirely justified and understandable. But not only did it cause death and misery for families, it helped 'prove' that this was the apocalypse and that the Devil was stalking the land with his handmaidens – witches.

8 Put to the horn

To be put to the horn was to be publicly denounced as a rebel. It meant the loss of name and status for the individual and placed the miscreant literally outside the law. This removal of the protection of the law thus gave everyone else the freedom to attack, imprison and even kill the individual with impunity. Outlaws were considered to be outwith the normal sphere of society and individuals were forbidden from rendering them assistance in any form. Helping an outlaw with food, clothing, shelter or any other form of aid could result in a fine, a whipping or imprisonment.

Society was, at that time, controlled by a variety of rules and laws emanating from church law, common law and the obligations and responsibilities due between the different sectors of society, ie the nobility, the middling folks and the poor. These various laws were held together by a general acceptance by all of certain moral norms. Crimes when they happened were punished and those who had been mistreated could seek redress. Those who had committed a crime would be punished but even during their punishment they were still part of society. Once their punishment was over, they could, with some exceptions, return to their normal life. To be put 'outwith' the law was to be cut off from society with no hope of return. This stemmed from the notion of perjury.

In early Scottish society, as was common in most European countries, an individual was only as good as his word. Society could only function with a basic level of trust. Bread bought from a baker contained the trust that the baker had not adulterated the flour. A cow bought from a farmer carried the trust that the cow would give good milk. If, therefore, an individual broke his word that trust was gone and society itself was under threat. In addition, if an individual broke his word then this was an affront to God who knew the secrets of all men's hearts.

Originally, being put to the horn had started as a means of enforcing debtors to pay their creditors. Rather than face gaol, a debtor would pledge an oath before God to pay his debts. If the debtor broke his oath, he became liable to the discipline of the Kirk as an oath-breaker or perjurer. The civil authorities would then issue 'letters of horning' denouncing the individual as a rebel against God. A messenger-at-arms would be sent to the main market town of the debtor's home parish and give three blasts with a horn before heralding the judgment of outlawry. This could result in the imprisonment of a named individual and the confiscation of his goods. As time went on, refusal to answer a court summons, which was issued in the name of the King, was also considered to be the breaking of an oath and thus would result in the individual being put to the horn.

It was frequently used against the Border reivers. Individuals thought guilty of various offences would be summoned before a sheriff to answer for their behaviour. Refusal to comply with the summons was tantamount to contempt of the King's authority and would result in the individual being declared outlaw.

9 The reivers[104]

The reivers were raiders from both sides of the Borders who lived by plunder, wreaking havoc from around the late 13th century to the 16th century. The reivers arose because of a combination of war, geography and old law.

From the late Middle Ages, Scotland and England had frequently been at war, with the Borders bearing the brunt of battles and the devastating effects of armies. Central authority was somewhat tenuous across the Anglo-Scottish border lands, as it was in the Anglo-Welsh border further south, and communities frequently felt uncertainty, fear and anxiety. Moreover, the central authorities that should have been maintaining law and order were the very ones that were causing the disruption. The only reliable source of security became the immediate family and tight-knit local community. Loyalty came, therefore, to be invested in the head of a family rather than to the civil or royal authorities who ruled the land in name only.

The rural Borders land, with the exception of areas such as Berwickshire, is predominantly marginal land such as open moorland. It is suitable only as grazing land with a subsequent predominance of livestock farming. However, this open moorland with livestock is difficult to protect and easy to raid. Kye and sheep can easily be stolen and the raiders and livestock disappear into the landscape.

The Borders was also an area that practised 'Gravelkind' inheritance, an old law which dictated that a man's land be divided equally between all of his sons. This law prevented the jealousy and potential bloodshed that could arise between sons in the Primogeniture system where the firstborn legitimate son inherits his entire estate. However, it led to ever diminishing parcels of land which, in the harsh environment of the Borders, were insufficient to maintain a household.

This combination of uncertainty, loyalty to the family heidsman and poor opportunities to sustain farming led to raiding or 'reiving' as a method of providing for one's family. Kye and sheep would be stolen in the autumn in order to sustain a family over the coming winter months.

But what started out as a method of survival soon developed into a system of raids and counter raids as other reiving families would launch more raids in retaliation. This then escalated until reivers attacked rival families and innocent communities alike. Men were murdered, women raped, kye stolen and houses put to the torch. With no recognition of the border or of the law on either side, the reivers rode with impunity. Disrespectful of the authority of both Scottish and English crowns, they knew only allegiance to their heidsman and family. Their society developed such that the authorities in Edinburgh and London came close to washing their hands of the entire region. Both authorities blamed the other for the situation and during the worst of the reiving days, some in both London and Edinburgh suggested moving the border to try and remove the problem from their jurisdiction. The border stayed put but the southern part of the Borders and north Northumbria were designated the 'debatable lands', wardens were posted to keep the peace with little hope of success and far less protection for local communities.

Eventually the rule of law and the weariness of many of the reiving families, who had fought each other to exhaustion, saw the reiving way of life start to wane. The union of the crowns and subsequent strengthening of the law saw the final end of the reivers but their influence would be felt in the Borders long into the 17th century. The Kirk knew full well the lack of respect shown to authority by the reiving families and knew how insidious such a notion could be. The flagrant lack of respect offered to the law could also be shown to the Kirk. And it was that legacy that the Kirk feared. In ordinary communities, however, while the dawning of the new century appeared to offer the promise of no more nightly raids, no more burnings, how could they be sure? The authorities in Edinburgh had failed to protect them before and so, when trouble struck, Borderers knew better than to expect any help. In many Borders witch trials, there was little contact with the authorities in Edinburgh except what was absolutely necessary. The Borders looked after its own.

10 Witches and healers

Contrary to the popular misconception, very few of those accused of being witches in Scotland were recorded as midwives or healers. In the Scottish records that exist, the occupations of accused witches only have around 4 per cent listed as either midwives or healers.

Medicine in the 17th century was divided between doctors, who treated the wealthy, and local remedies that would be applied, in most instances, by the mother in the home. Illness could result from many sources, most of which were poorly understood and beliefs around illness and healing were intimately bound up in beliefs in the supernatural. This was even facilitated by the Kirk as the church had a long history of seeing illness as a punishment from God for sin. The Black Death was blamed on the sinfulness of Man in general but particularly on sinful women that did not know their place!

As always with the Kirk, there was a double standard. Praying to God for forgiveness for sin to remove illness or praying to the Virgin to help with infertility was allowed. Going to the local healer who might use herbs and potions but also charms and spells was not. However innocent the charm may have been, after the Reformation, the Kirk heard diabolical spells and papist beliefs – in their eyes the same thing – rather than heavenly pleas for help and cried witch.

Mortality rates were high and even in years of plenty food and no plague, life expectancy for ordinary individuals was about 40 years. Around 25 per cent of children died before their first birthday and 50 per cent died before their tenth birthday. Childbirth was an especially dangerous time for women with approximately 200 out of every 1,000 births resulting in a maternal death. Illness and childbirth were women's work with older female relatives such as grandmothers helping to deliver babies and attending to sick children. They were frequently present when illness occurred and thus an easy target to blame, when death occurred. Of those accused of causing the illness or death of a child by witchcraft, the vast majority were relatives that had merely been helping with herbal remedies and a homely prayer in a family crisis rather than formal healers.

For men working out in the field, there were added hazards from farm tools and animals or when moving rocks and trees. A graze that became infected could result in sepsis and death; a broken leg badly splinted might cripple an individual for life. Where injury did occur it was, yet again, older female family members that cared for the injured man.

Older women would, therefore, at some point in their lives have acted as healers and midwives but may not have been healers and midwives by occupation or have stopped being a healer or midwife by the time of their arrest. Thus the arrest warrants did not record them as healers. But older women who had possibly outlived their family, who may have talked to themselves or muttered old rhymes under their breath were on the fringes of society and were easy prey for accusations. In addition, the Kirk's portrayal of them as witches suited the propaganda that the Devil was a liar and a trickster and if you followed him you did not become rich but remained poor. The reality of successful middling folk and members of the nobility who followed the Devil was not one that the Kirk wanted known.

Appendix B

The Scottish witch trials: numbers and locations

BETWEEN 1590 AND 1722, around 3,937 witch trials were carried in Scotland. This number comes from existing records. While these are probably the majority of cases, new records continue to be found and, although the final figure may never be known, it may possibly be greater than 4,000.

The records of witchcraft cases are frustratingly piecemeal in many cases. George Black's *Calendar of Cases of Witchcraft in Scotland 1510 to 1727* in combination with Larner, Hyde Lee and McLachlan's *Source book of Scottish Witchcraft* list many of the known cases. The most comprehensive database of trial records was compiled by Edinburgh University between 2001 and 2003 although new records continue to be uncovered.

Around 16 per cent of those tried in Scotland as witches were men; the figure in the Borders was lower – around eight per cent or some 28 of those in the existing records.

Number of witchcraft trials

	Number
Banff, Angus and Kincardine	183
The Borders	352
Central Scotland	297
Edinburgh and the Lothians[1]	922
Fife	323
Galloway	248
Grampian including Aberdeen	257
Highlands and Islands	204
Orkney and Shetland	87
Stratclyde and the West	342
Unknown areas	625

[1] Shipping area and capital, contained the High Courts and so
drew in cases from across the entire country.

Appendix C

The Border witch trials:
numbers tried and locations

WHILE THE POPULATION of early modern Scotland was more evenly distributed than it is today, the Borders was still a relatively sparsely populated area. As such, the number of trials is much higher than would be anticipated. Strathclyde and the West, Central Scotland and Grampian were all more populous that the Borders but had far fewer trials.

Fate of the Border Witches

	Executed	Other punishment	Acquitted	Diet deserted	Unknown fate	Total
Ayton	7	1	-	-	4	12
Annan	-	-	-	-	1	1
Berwickshire	26	3	-	-	6	35
Chirnshire	-	2	-	-	2	4
Cockburnspath	1	-	-	-	1	2
Coldingham	10	-	-	-	5	15
Coldstream	8	-	-	-	3	11
Duns	8	-	1	-	5	14
Earlston	-	-	-	-	2	2
Eyemouth	24	2	2	-	6	34
Fountainhall	-	-	-	-	1	1
Galashiels	5	-	-	-	4	9
Greenlaw	-	-	-	-	2	2
Heriot	-	-	-	-	1	1
Innerleithen	3	1	-	-	2	6
Jedburgh	23	1	3	-	8	35
Kelso	12	3	-	-	1	16
Lauder	7	-	-	-	8	15
Lilliesleaf	1	-	-	-	3	4
Melrose	16	2	-	-	1	19
Moffat	-	-	-	-	2	2
Paxton	-	-	-	-	3	3
Peebles	41	8	1	-	11	61
Romano	-	-	-	-	1	1
Roxburgh	3	4	-	-	2	9
Selkirk	20	2	-	-	5	27
Stobo	-	-	-	2	1	3
Stow	6	-	-	-	1	7
Tranquair	-	-	-	-	1	1
Total	221	29	7	2	93	352[1]

[1] This number records the 352 known individuals tried. Due to the incomplete nature of the records, it cannot be verified the exact number of witches tried in those 352 trials. (These numbers come from existing records. The true number may possibly be higher.)

Appendix D
Places to visit

Coldingham

Church of Scotland parish church houses the remains of Coldingham Priory.

Eyemouth

The cliffs to the west of the town where Elizabeth Bathgate was said to sink ships.

Jedburgh

The Jed water at Allerley Well Park. The probable site where Mary Somerville's body was dumped.

Lauder

The 19th century townhall is the site of the 17th century tolbooth where the Lauder witches were tried.

Peebles

Tor Hill. The site where the Peebles witches were said to hold their meetings.

Selkirk

The Auld Kirk. Where the minister preached against witches.

Stobo

The Auld Kirk. Where the minister preached against witches.

Stow

The packhorse bridge. The site of the Stow witch executions.

Appendix E

Trace your ancestors

THERE ARE THREE main ways to check to see if your ancestors were involved in any witchcraft cases. Not all trial records have survived but you may also find note of your ancestor in old parish records.

1. Using the University of Edinburgh's interactive database you can find the names of those accused of witchcraft as well as those who sat at commissioners in the trial. www.witches.shca.ed.ac.uk/

2. The National Records of Scotland. Their archives may be accessed online or in person at the National Records building in Edinburgh. www.nrscotland.gov.uk/

3. The Heritage Hub: Scottish Borders Archive and Local History Centre. Their archives may be accessed online or in person at the Heritage building in Hawick. www.calmview.eu/HUBCAT/CalmView/

Bibliography

Black, George. F., *Calendar of Cases of Witchcraft in Scotland 1510 to 1727* (New York: Kessinger Publishing, 2000)

Brown, N.P., *Pagans and Priests* (Oxford: Lion Hudson, 2006)

Calvin, Jean., *Institutes of the Christian Religion* (1536)

Cantor, N.F., *In the Wake of the Plague* (London: Simon & Schuster UK Ltd, 2001)

Cawthorne, N., *Witch Hunt* (London: Arcturus Publishing Ltd, 2002)

Chambers, Robert., *Domestic Annals of Scotland* (Edinburgh and London: Chambers, 1859–61)

Craig-Brown, Thomas., *History of Selkirkshire* (1886)

Davidson, T., *Rowan Tree and Red Thread* (Edinburgh: Oliver and Boyd, 1949)

Dumville, David N., 'Nennius and the "Historia Brittonum"' in: Studia Celtica, 10/11 (1975/6)

Ewan, E & Meickle, M. (eds.), *Women in Scotland, c.1100–c.1750* (East Lothian: Tuckwell Press, 1999)

The Fraser Manuscript., *A Collection of Providential Passages Antient and Modern Forreign and Domestick* (Edinburgh 1670)

Goodare, J., *The Scottish Witch-hunt in Context* (Manchester: Manchester University Press, 2002)

Kramer, H., *Malleus Maleficarum* (1486) (ed) Maxwell-Stuart, P.G., (Manchester: Manchester University Press, 2007)

Jillings, K., *Scotland's Black Death* (Stroud: Tempus Publishing Limited, 2003)

Knox, J., *The First Blast of the Trumpet against the Monstrous Regiment of Women* (1558)

Kors, A.C., Peters, E., *Witchcraft in Europe 400–1700* (Philadelphia: University of Pennsylvania Press, 2001)

Lamont-Brown, R., *Scottish Witchcraft* (Edinburgh: Chambers, 1994)

Larner, C., *Enemies of God* (London: Chatto & Windus, 1981)

Larner, C., Hyde Lee, C., McLachlan, H., *Source book of Scottish Witchcraft* (Glasgow: The Grimsay Press, 2005)

Linton, E. L., *Witch Stories* (London: Chapman and Hall, 1861)

MacKenzie, Kirsteen, M., *The Solemn League and Covenant of the Three Kingdoms and the Cromwellian Union, 1643–1663* (London: Routledge, 2017)

Maidment, J., *Spottiswoode Miscellany Vol ii* (Edinburgh, 1845)

Marshall, K., *John Knox* (Edinburgh: Birlinn Limited, 2000)

Maxwell-Stuart, P.G., *An Abundance of Witches* (Stroud: Tempus Publishing Limited, 2005)

Maxwell-Stuart, P.G., *Satan's Conspiracy* (East Lothian: Tuckwell Press, 2001)

Maxwell-Stuart, P.G., *Witchcraft A History* (Stroud: Tempus Publishing Limited, 2000)

Maxwell-Stuart, P.G., *Witch Hunters* (Stroud: Tempus Publishing Limited, 2003)

Moffat, A., *The Reivers* (Edinburgh: Birlinn Limited, 2007)

Normand, L., & Roberts, G., *Witchcraft in Early Modern Scotland* (Exeter: University of Exeter Press, 2000)

Scott, G.R., *A History of Torture* (London: Senate Publishing, 1994)

Scott, Hew., *Fasti Ecclesiae Scoticanae: The Succession of Ministers in the Church of Scotland from the Reformation* (Edinburgh: Oliver and Boyd, 1915)

Scott, W., *Letters on Demonology and Witchcraft* (Hertfordshire: Wordsworth Editions Limited, 2001)

Stuart, J., *Daemonologie* (Edinburgh, 1591) eds Normand, L., and Roberts G., (Exeter: University of Exeter Press, 2000)

Wedgewood, C.V., *The Thirty Years War* (New York: New York Review of Books, 2005)

Young, J. R., 'The Covenanters and the Scottish Parliament, 1639–51: the rule of the godly and the 'second Scottish Reformation', E. Boran and C. Gribben, eds, *Enforcing Reformation in Ireland and Scotland, 1550–1700* (Aldershot: Ashgate, 2006)

Sources

1) Manuscript Sources
   British History Online
   www.british-history.ac.uk
   The Heritage Hub: Scottish Borders Archive and Local History
   Centre
   www.calmview.eu/HUBCAT/CalmView/
   The National Library of Scotland, Edinburgh www.nls.uk
   The National Records of Scotland, Edinburgh www.nrscotland.
   gov.uk
   Scottish Archive Network www.scan.org.uk

2) Database Sources
   Julian Goodare, Lauren Martin, Joyce Miller and Louise
   Yeoman, 'The Survey of Scottish Witchcraft', www.arts.ed.ac.
   uk/witches/ (accessed April–June 2019)

3) Other Sources
   BBC Radio Scotland Witch Hunt podcast, www.bbc.co.uk/
   programmes/p07rn38z/episodes/downloads

Endnotes

1. Halsall, Paul., Innocent VIII: BULL Summis Desiderantes, Dec. 5th, 1484, *Medieval Sourcebook*, Fordham University
2. Calvin, J., *Institutes of the Christian Religion* (1536)
3. MacKenzie, Kirsteen, M., *The Solemn League and Covenant of the Three Kingdoms and the Cromwellian Union, 1643-1663* (2017)
4. Knox, J., *The First Book of Discipline* (1560)
5. Knox, J., *The First Blast of the Trumpet against the Monstrous Regiment of Women* (1558)
6. Knox, J., *The Second Book of Discipline* (1564)
7. Wedgewood, C.V., *The Thirty Years War* (1938)
8. Acts of the General Assembly of the Church of Scotland 1638–1842
9. Register of the Privy Council, 2nd series, vol.3, p.170
10. ibid., p.391
11. ibid., p.391
12. Kramer, H., *Malleus maleficarum* (1486)
13. Record of the Privy Council, 2nd series, vol.3, p.270
14. ibid., p.238
15. ibid., p.239
16. Records of the Parliament of Scotland, 1643/6/1
17. Records of the Regality of Melrose, 1605-1661, v.1, p.220.
18. *Newes from Scotland,* 1591 (1816, London) British Library C.101.a.6.
19. Normand, L. and Roberts G., (eds) *Witchcraft in Early Modern Scotland: James VI's* Daemonologie (Exeter: University of Exeter Press, 2000)
20. Register of the Privy Council, 2nd series, vol.3, p.378
21. ibid., pp.381–82
22. ibid., vol.3, p.361
23. ibid., vol.4, p.15
24. ibid., vol.3, pp.397–400
25. ibid., vol.4, p.98
26. ibid., vol.4, p.131
27. ibid., vol.3, p.443
28. Scottish Justiciary Court VI, p.143
29. ibid., p.147
30. Register of Royal Letters, Vol 1, p.377, Vol 2, pp.418; 553
31. ibid., vol.5, pp.176–77

32. ibid., vol.5, pp.176–77
33. ibid., vol.5, pp.176–77
34. ibid., vol.5, pp.176–77
35. ibid., vol.5, p.572
36. ibid., vol.5, pp.605–6
37. *The discovery of witches*, 1649
38. Dumville, David N. (1975) Nennius and the "Historia Brittonum". pp.78–95
39. Published in 1910 by the Benedictine monk Michael Barnett. Origin unknown.
40. History of Selkirkshire, v.1, p.451
41. CH2/338/2, Stow Parish Kirk Session, June 1649
42. Stow Parish Kirk Session, June 1649
43. ibid.
44. Register of the Privy Council, 2nd series, vol.4, pp.427; 433
45. CH2/185/6, p.123 Haddington Presbytery Records
46. Register of the privy Council, 3rd series, vol.1, p.251
47. ibid., vol.1, p.252
48. ibid., vol.1, p.252
49. ibid., vol 1, p.210
50. ibid., vol.1, p.224
51. Committee of Estates PA11/8fo.172r
52. ibid.
53. ibid.
54. ibid.
55. ibid.
56. ibid.
57. ibid.
58. *A Collection of Providential Passages Antient and Modern Forreign and Domestick,* pp. 307–312
59. *A Collection of Providential Passages Antient and Modern Forreign and Domestick,* pp. 307–312
60. Register of the Privy Council, 3rd series, vol 1, p.221
61. ibid., p.221
62. Gibson, Marion (2006), 'Witchcraft in the Courts', in Gibson, Marion (ed.), *Witchcraft And Society in England And America, 1550–1750,* Continuum International Publishing Group, pp.1–9
63. *Newes from Scotland,* 1591 (1816, London) British Library C.101.a.6.
64. Register of the Privy Council, 2nd series, vol.3, pp.41–42
65. *Spottiswoode Miscellany*, vol.2, pp.90–91
66. Register of the Privy Council, 3rd series, vol.1, p.237
67. *Spottiswoode Miscellany*, v.2, p.167
68. Register of the Privy Council, 3rd series, vol.3, p.101
69. *Spottiswoode Miscellany*, v.2, p.271

70. ibid., v.2, p.271
71. Register of the Privy Council, 3rd series, vol.3, p.101
72. Acts of the Parliament of Scotland, vol. 3, p.44
73. Book of the Universall Kirk, Vol 1, pp.343–4
74. SRO, JC2/14, pp.259–260
75. Scottish Poor Roll, National Records of Scotland, CH1 series
76. Acts of the Scottish Parliament, 1587, National Records of Scotland, PA1-3 series
77. Young, J. R., *The Covenanters and the Scottish Parliament, 1639–51: the rule of the godly and the second Scottish Reformation*, pp.149–50
78. Circuit Court Books, JC10/2 fo. 210r
79. Records of the Justiciary court of Edinburgh, v.2, p.56
80. High Court Process Notes JC2/13f.76v
81. Circuit Court Book JC 10/2 fo. 210r
82. High Court Process Notes, JC2/13
83. ibid.
84. ibid., JC26/38
85. Circuit Court Books JC10/3 fo.26v.,50r
86. ibid.
87. Chamber, *Domestic Annals*, v.5, pp.240
88. Black, George F., *Calendar of Cases of Witchcraft in Scotland 1510 to 1727*
89. Register of the Privy Council, 2nd series, vol. 3, p.270
90. *Fasti Ecclesiae Scoticanae*, p.418
91. Black, George.F., *Calendar*, p.47
92. ibid., p.62
93. ibid., p.76
94. ibid., p.78
95. ibid., p.82
96. Act of the British Parliament, 1735
97. Craig-Brown, T., *History of Selkirkshire*, v.2, p.100
98. ibid., p.100
99. Register of the Privy Council, 3rd series, vol.1, p.141
100. Craig-Brown, T., *History of Selkirkshire*, v.2, p.100
101. Moffat, A., *The Reivers*
102. Reinhard Tenberg (1990), 'Institoris, Heinrich', in Bautz, Friedrich Wilhelm (ed.), *Biographisch-Bibliographisches Kirchenlexikon (BBKL)* Hamm: Bautz. cols. 1307–1310
103. *The Bulk of the Chronicles of Scotland*, William Stewart Vol III, p.373
104. Moffat, A., *The Reivers* (2017)

Some other books published by **LUATH** PRESS

Agnes Finnie
The Witch of the Potterrow Port
Mary W Craig
ISBN 9781804250198 PBK £9.99

AGNES
FINNIE

The Witch of the Potterrow Port

MARY W. CRAIG

She has been commonlie called a rank witch these many years bygane
The trial of Agnes Finnie, kirk session of Greyfriars 1644

Agnes Finnie's story is much more nuanced and more interesting than that of the stereotypical poor defence-less woman persecuted by the Kirk. Through Agnes' story, the everyday lives of ordinary people struggling to survive are revealed. Scotland became increasingly seen as a land under threat from the Devil and his handmaidens: witches. The women and men who were accused of witchcraft were real people with real lives. This is just one of their stories.

During the 17th century when witch hunts were a daily occurrence, if a woman was arrested and accused of being a witch she would be tried and usually found guilty in a matter of days, even hours. This was not the case for Agnes, a working woman living in the tenements of Edinburgh. Her whole trial was unusual. It took months of deliberation from the jury.

Mary W. Craig explores Agnes' curious case and provides a fascinating insight into the political and religious tensions that led to Agnes' burning.

The Boy, The Witch and The Queen of Scots

Barbara Henderson

ISBN 9781804251317 PBK £7.99

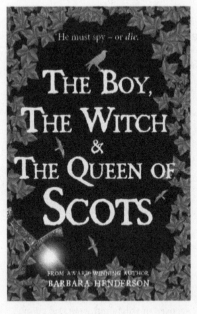

No.
Not the Palace.
Anywhere but the Palace.

12-year-old Alexander Buchan was once content, training as a falconer at Strathbogie Castle in Huntly. But when his Earl sends him to Edinburgh to the court of the newly arrived Mary, Queen of Scots, the boy finds himself lured into a world of intrigue, terror and treachery. Alexander knows right from wrong, but how can he hope to outwit his master's murderous messenger'? Surely no one can defy an Earl – especially one whose wife is rumoured to be a witch!

Soon, more than the boy's own life is at stake: his friend Lizzie is arrested and the angry clouds of Reformation Scotland gather around the young Queen.

It seems that Alexander must spy – or die.

The Boy, The Witch & The Queen of Scots *is a thrilling, gripping historical adventure.*
SUSAN BROWNRIGG, Children's Author

A true gem in children's literature, The Boy, the Witch & The Queen of Scots *is a triumph that brings history to life in a way that both educates and entertains.*
MR RIPLEY, Blogger

The action started straight away which will hook children in.
RACHEL BRUCE, Teacher and Historian

A fascinating glimpse into the past – perfect for the primary classroom.
STEVEN KENYON, Teacher Educator for English and History

I was completely gripped by this page-turner! Barbara has tapped into a truly unique perspective of one of Scotland's most fascinating eras!
TRACY HARROWER-RENNIE, Teacher and Historian

Six Black Candles

Des Dillon

ISBN 9781906307493 PBK £8.99

Winner of the 2000 Television Arts Performance Showcase Writer of the Year Award, the 2001 International Festival of Playwriting Award and the 2004 Critics Award for Theatre in Scotland (Best Ensemble Play)

Caroline's husband abandons her (bad move) for Stacie Gracie, his assistant at the meat counter, and incurs more wrath than he anticipated. Caroline, her five sisters, mother and granny, all with a penchant for witchery, invoke the lethal spell of the Six Black Candles. A natural reaction to the break up of a marriage?

Set in present day Irish Catholic Coatbridge, Six Black Candles is bound together by the ropes of traditional storytelling and the strength of female familial relationships. Bubbling under the cauldron of superstition, witchcraft and religion is the heat of revenge; and the love and venom of sisterhood.

A darkly humorous and satanic fictional brew... written in vivid demonic style... with punchy directness and enormous brio.
SCOTLAND ON SUNDAY

Hilarious.
THE MIRROR

The author's humanity and the sense of real hardship are what make the novel.
THE BIG ISSUE

Entertaining and thought-provoking.
TIME OUT MOSCOW

A bitingly witty, funny novel from Des Dillon.
COSMOPOLITAN (Russia)

Testament of a Witch

Douglas Watt

ISBN 9781913025281 PBK £8.99

FEATURING
INVESTIGATIVE
ADVOCATE
JOHN MACKENZIE

DOUGLAS WATT
STAMENT OF A
WITCH

I confess that I am a witch. I have sold myself body and soul unto Satan. My mother took me to the Blinkbonny Woods where we met other witches. I put a hand on the crown of my head and the other on the sole of my foot. I gave everything between unto him.

1687. The nation is gripped by fear of witches and hunts are taking place all over the country. In Edinburgh, a young woman is accused of witchcraft, tortured with pins and sleep deprivation.

As John MacKenzie and his assistant Davie Scougall investigate her suspicious death, they find themselves in a village overwhelmed by superstition, resentment and puritanical religion. In this time of spiritual, political and social upheaval, will reason allow MacKenzie to reveal the true evil lurking in the town, before the witch-hunt claims yet another victim?

The Nine Maidens
Priestesses of the Ancient World
Stuart McHardy
ISBN 9781804250914 PBK £9.99

When King Arthur was conveyed to Avalon they were there.

When Odin summoned warriors to Valhalla they were there.

When Apollo was worshipped on Greek mountains they were there.

When Brendan came to the Island of Women they were there.

They are the Nine Maidens – from the mothers of the Norse God Heimdall, Morgan and her sisters on Avalon, to the nine sisters at the heart of the found myth of the Gikuyu of Kenya or witches battling with the Irish St Patrick, these women stand out in history and mythology.

Triggered by a local story still told in his native Dundee, Stuart McHardy has traced what seems to be memories of groups of nine women across much of Europe and as far as Siberia, Korea, India and Africa. Whether as Pictish saints, muses, valkyries, druidesses or witches, the tales of these groups of nine women transcend a vast range of cultural and linguistic boundaries.

McHardy's approach is richly rewarding because he encompasses a widening range of references to establish the rooted richness of the Nine Maidens motif in different cultural contexts.
CENCRASTUS

McHardy succeeds in demonstrating that our living culture in Scotland is older and more complex than we previously realised. Far from being an obscure side path, the Nine Maidens turns out to be remarkably pervasive. You may never look at familiar features of the Scottish landscape in the same way again.
DONALD SMITH

Details of these and other books published by Luath Press can be found at:
www.luath.co.uk

Luath Press Limited

committed to publishing well written books worth reading

LUATH PRESS takes its name from Robert Burns, whose little collie Luath (*Gael.*, swift or nimble) tripped up Jean Armour at a wedding and gave him the chance to speak to the woman who was to be his wife and the abiding love of his life. Burns called one of the 'Twa Dogs' Luath after Cuchullin's hunting dog in Ossian's *Fingal*.

Luath Press was established in 1981 in the heart of Burns country, and is now based a few steps up the road from Burns' first lodgings on Edinburgh's Royal Mile. Luath offers you distinctive writing with a hint of unexpected pleasures.

Most bookshops in the UK, the US, Canada, Australia, New Zealand and parts of Europe, either carry our books in stock or can order them for you. To order direct from us, please send a £sterling cheque, postal order, international money order or your credit card details (number, address of cardholder and expiry date) to us at the address below. Please add post and packing as follows: UK – £1.00 per delivery address; overseas surface mail – £2.50 per delivery address; overseas airmail – £3.50 for the first book to each delivery address, plus £1.00 for each additional book by airmail to the same address. If your order is a gift, we will happily enclose your card or message at no extra charge.

Luath Press Limited
543/2 Castlehill
The Royal Mile
Edinburgh EH1 2ND
Scotland
Telephone: +44 (0)131 225 4326 (24 hours)
Email: sales@luath. co.uk
Website: www. luath.co.uk